THE THREE PATHS

AND

DHARMA

THE THREE PATHS

AND

DHARMA

ANNIE BESANT

GYAN

Published by

GYAN

Gyan Publishing House
5, Ansari Road
Daryaganj, New Delhi-110002
Phone: 011-47034999, 9811692060
E-mail: books@gyanbooks.com

Distribution Network
gyanbooks.com
India, USA, Canada, UK, Australia

ISBN: 978-93-6780-414-8 (PB)

First Published, 1897

2nd Impression 2024

Printed at: Gyan Press, Delhi.

THE THREE PATHS AND DHARMA
Author: ANNIE BESANT

THE THREE PATHS

AND

DHARMA

THE THREE PATHS

AND

DHARMA

BY

ANNIE BESANT

SECOND EDITION

THEOSOPHICAL PUBLISHING SOCIETY
LONDON
1902

PREFACE TO THE ENGLISH EDITION

THIS little book appeals, perhaps, to the eastern rather than to the western type of mind, but so many souls trained in the East are now being reincarnated in the West that it may find friendly readers away from the land of its birth. Addressed to a purely Hindu audience, the lectures contain many common Samskrit words, familiar to every Hindu, that may sound strange in the ears of readers of other faiths; but it seems better to retain them, for those who object to them will object to the whole eastern colouring of the booklet, and the changing of a few words would not shape the lectures to meet their views. To some it will carry a message deeper and sweeter than the more conventional and colder West is yet ready to welcome. For such souls it was spoken; let others pass it by.

ANNIE BESANT.

CONTENTS

THE THREE PATHS

(TO UNION WITH GOD)

Lectures delivered at Benares, at the Sixth Annual Convention of the Indian Section of the Theosophical Society, October 19th, 20th, and 21st, 1896

FOREWORD

On the occasion of the Sixth Annual Convention of the Indian Section of the Theosophical Society I was asked to deliver three lectures and to take the *Bhagavad Gîtâ* as subject. Feeling quite incompetent to lecture on that divine book, I took the humbler topic of the Three Paths of Karma, Gnyâna, and Bhakti, as explained in the *Bhagavad Gîtâ*, and the lectures delivered are now issued in book-form.

I am indebted to Babu Sirish Chandra Bose, Munsif, of Benares, for the wonderfully accurate report which he most kindly took of the discourses; I have been reported by the best London men, but have never sent a report to the Press with less correction than that supplied by my amateur friend.

ANNIE BESANT.

BENARES,
February 1, 1897.

THE THREE PATHS

KARMA MÂRGA

THREE Paths have been traced by the Sages, along any one of which a man may tread, and, by following, may attain liberation. Three are the Paths, and yet in a sense they are but one. Differing in their methods, their end is one and the same. Differing in the external conditions, they all lead to the one Self, they all seek the same goal. These three Paths—the three Mârgas as they are called in the Indian Philosophy—that of Karma or action, that of Gnyâna or Wisdom, that of Bhakti or Devotion—these three Paths finally blend into one, each of them acquiring in the end the qualities of the others, each of them passing as it were into the other two, blending into one the characteristics of the three. For when you reach Yoga, whether it be the Karma Yoga, or whether it be the Gnyâna Yoga, or whether it be the Bhakti Yoga, the end is one—Union with the Self; the attributes needed resemble each other, and the man reaching perfection through one is wanting in none of the qualities which have been developed along any of the three Paths.

These three Paths, in the difference of their methods, and in the identity of their aim, have been explained for us in that most beautiful and most widely spread of Indian Scriptures, the Song of the Lord, the Discourse of Shrî Krishna —the *Bhagavad Gîtâ*. There it is that the Paths are explained, and there it is that their end is declared. There we learn how in the heart of the man of perfect devotion wisdom springs up; there we learn how action may be wrought without attachment, without binding a man to rebirth; and there we learn also that along any one of these Paths the Lord will meet with man, the Supreme will bless him. Let men travel along one or the other, they seek the one Self whether by action, or by wisdom, or by devotion; and those who seek shall surely, shall inevitably, find Him; for the Self of all is One, and the goal of the three Paths is the same.

If we turn our glance over Nature, if we look over the whole of the world, everywhere we find things seeking the Self; everywhere in every direction, under whatever form and whatever name, whether wisely or blindly, whether clear-sightedly or gropingly, all seek the Self, all are striving to find the Self. The sun as it darts its rays through space is seeking the Self; the vast ocean when it surges into waves is but seeking the Self; the winds as they wander over the surface of the earth are seeking the Self; the forest trees as they stretch their arms outwards are seeking the Self; every animal, however dimly, is groping after the Self; mankind, however blindly, however foolishly, however mistakenly, is searching for the Self. This tendency in all creation, this universal fact in every form of life, in ancient times was called the seeking of the Self. Modern science notices the same tendency in Nature, and names it Evolution. So to whichever side we turn, ancient or modern, we find this upward, this inward, aspiration.

Why should all things seek the Self? Why should the Self be the goal of all endeavours? Is it not because the Self dwells alike in the hearts of all? Whether it be in the ocean, whether it be in a mineral or in a tree, whether in an animal or in a man, the Self there is hidden within, concealed by the outer covering of illusion. The one Self is seated alike in the sun and in the cavity of the heart, and every living creature searching after happiness is but seeking the Self; for searching, however mistakenly, after happiness is but the blind groping after the Self which is Bliss. Yea, the Self is Bliss, eternal, unending, undying; and what we call happiness is the Self, which is Bliss reflected in broken beams through the medium which surrounds us. Let none mistake, let none be blinded by the divergences of seeking, by the errors caused by the outer illusions; for all are really seeking in the outer form the inner life. They seek it everywhere, in all their blind efforts after joy; and it was the Self Incarnate, Shrî Krishna, who said: "Who seeth seated equally in all beings the supreme Îshvara, he seeth." *

The Paths that we are to trace in these afternoon meetings are the three great Paths along which consciously or unconsciously the Self is sought. In the earlier stages the seeking is unconscious seeking, the blind desire for happiness, for satisfaction and joy. In the later stages the seeking becomes conscious, an intelligent understanding of what is sought, and of the methods of the search. Whether in blindness or in vision, the search is being carried on, and according to the stage of the evolution of the soul is its knowledge of the methods and its knowledge of its final goal. These Paths as they are followed raise the man above the illusion caused by the qualities of Nature, those qualities known to us in their widest sense as the three guṇas. It is these that blind the souls, that veil the Self, that bring

* *Bhagavad Gitâ*, xiii. 27.

in the character of illusion and prevent the recognition of the reality. On the Paths men learn, by utilising these very guṇas, to rise beyond them, using different methods—of activity, of wisdom, and of devotion—in order to learn to separate the Self from the outer activities, to learn to discriminate the Self from the senses and the mind which move after their appropriate objects, to pass above and beyond the guṇas; and then, above and beyond the guṇas, they find the unveiled Self.

The Path that is our special object of study this afternoon is Karma Mârga, the Path of Action, which is blindly and quite unconsciously followed by the mass of mankind, not knowing either the method or the object. We shall find, as we look into the history of our race, that this Karma Mârga leads man to plunge into action of every kind, to rush out after objects of every description, to go restlessly seeking satisfaction by way of the external universe, always trying to get more and more and more, always to accumulate more and more largely, and, chiefly by increasing activity, by greater energy of motion, by increased concentration of effort, by incessant action, to find the Self. He plunges into action, saying, "I do, I feel, I experience, I have pleasure and pain." He knows not that all these doings, feelings, experiences of pleasure and pain, belong to the energies of Nature, and that the true Self is not doing, nor feeling, nor acting; that these energies of Nature are following one eternal, ceaseless round. At first he is moved to action by desire for its fruit. He desires to enjoy. If he lies down doing nothing, without activity, he will feel no enjoyment, he will constantly suffer; the body itself would perish were utter inactivity to supervene. Tamas has first to be overcome; the quality in Nature of darkness, sluggishness, inertia, sloth, has to be mastered, controlled, and brought into entire subjection. Look at the mass of mankind and see how little at present they are susceptible to higher impulses. It would be useless to appeal to their desire for knowledge, for they have no such longing. They cannot appreciate the delights of intellectual struggle, still less can they answer to the stimulus of spiritual aspiration. They are sunk in the darkness of the tâmasic guṇa, are wrapped in ignorance and in darkness, and desire to remain undisturbed. How shall they be stirred into activity? Better activity of any kind than no activity at all; better misdirected energy than absolute inertia—the absence of all motion. They must be moved. At first the grossest and the coarsest animal desires are the spurs of Nature, the sting, as it were, of Nature's whip, driving the sluggish beings into exertion, and scourging them forth on the path of action. Man must be moved by desires, by something to which his nature responds. Later on these desires will be recognised as degrading, as unworthy of humanity, as dragging him back on the Path, as stifling higher possibilities. But in the earlier stages they are necessary for the growth of man, for his progress out of this tâmasic quality which enwraps him, which prevents him from moving at all. They are better than death ; low as they are, they have more promise in them than absolute stagnation. So the activity which is born of desire, which stirs the man to action, which makes him seek gratification, which sends him after pleasure even though the pleasure be low, is the early teaching of Nature which drives him into activity in order that he may grow. However much then these evils are to be reprobated, they have their place, their function for the lowest and most stagnant natures. And therefore the Lord has said that He is present even in the vices of the vicious, in that which is driving them into action in order that some activity may be obtained.

Treading the Path of Karma, the man later on is moved by a desire for a somewhat higher fruit, and that develops in him the quality of Rajas. He becomes exceedingly active ; he rushes out in every direction. His energies are abundant, overwhelming, aggressive, and combative. He flies into the outer world, driven by the activities of the senses and the mind, and seeking their gratification. He performs action with this desire for fruit.

Now the fruit may be of two kinds. He desires to enjoy the result of his action, whether it may be in this world, or whether it may happen to be in another. If we glance back to ages which are known to be less material, if we look backward to the times when religion was exercising a predominant influence over mankind, when man recognised the immortality of the soul, not as a phrase of the lips but as the ruling idea of the life, when the man felt and knew that he himself was immortal, then the action was motived by the desire for fruit to be enjoyed in the realms of Svarga. The man's activities might be râjasic, working entirely for fruit, giving up a thing here that he might gain much more elsewhere; sacrificing some of his wealth in charity in order that he might have goods on the other side of death; laying up happiness in the super-physical realm, that in Svarga he might enjoy the fruit; yet in those ages, though the action was largely guided by the motive or desire for fruit, the fruit was to be enjoyed in the realms on the other side of death, instead of being limited to the material delights of the earth.

But if we turn to the activities around us at the present time, to the Path as it is being trodden so very largely in the West, and to an increasing extent in the East, we shall find that the fruit of action that men are desiring, the fruit which is the motive of their exertion and the object of their labour, that fruit is to be something on this side of death, and consists very largely in the increase of material objects, in the acquirement and the possession of material wealth. Let us look now for a moment at the western nations. We find them continually engaged in the effort to increase their comforts. I may call it, in fact, a diseased activity. No man is thought to be doing anything unless there is a result produced on the physical material plane. The activity is not recognised unless it bring fruit in the physical, in the outer or lower material world. You find men very often following science. While the desire on the part of the scientific discoverer may be the desire for knowledge pure and simple, the interest of the public in his discovery, the eagerness with which they watch his progress, the great anxiety with which they take up his results, is because the increase of knowledge leads to increased power for the accumulation of objects, to increased gratification of material desires, to increased abundance of material wealth. We find endless multiplication of objects. There is a race between the objects that gratify desires and the creation of new desires which will demand fresh objects for their gratification. There is a constant struggle between the wearied men of the world, of wealth, and of pleasure, who are longing for new sensations, for new activities, for new channels into which all their energies may pour, and those who supply their desires, who try to invent new objects in order to stimulate fresh desires and thus obtain fresh avenues of employment for themselves. Thus always men want to have more and more pleasures of the same kind. Men have learned to travel faster; journeys that used to take formerly the greater part perhaps of a year are now accomplished in a month or so, and journeys of months are accomplished in weeks or even in days. But is man very much the happier, and has his desire been satisfied? No. His cry to the man of science still is: "Find us a new motive power, something that will transcend the possibilities of steam, something like electricity if you will, which will enable us to cross continents and oceans in a couple of days, and fly over the surface of earth with greater rapidity. Steam we are tired of; find electricity, or find some new motor that will carry us more swiftly."

How much is man really the happier for this swifter movement? How much would he be the higher in spiritual progress if he could do in a day what before he took a year to do? More and more speed, bigger and bigger vessels, and thus men go on in an unending succession. Lately they were boasting in the papers in Paris that a new man will come into existence on a new earth, because they hope to create food by chemical processes instead of by agricultural methods, because they are getting more knowledge, accumulating greater stores of wealth. That pursuit is doomed to failure. That restless seeking for satisfaction in mere increase of activity has no ending. More and more may be gained; more and more may be accumulated; and, in the midst of it all, man will remain weary and discontented, because in none of these is the Self to be found unveiled, and the soul of man, identical in nature with the Self, is ever weary until it finds its home in Him. Therefore it is that along that particular line of karma no ultimate satisfaction can be gained. A man toils all his life for wealth, but he is discontented, and in the midst of all his possessions the cry is for something more. Truly was it said by Manu that we might as well try to extinguish a fire by pouring butter into it, as to extinguish desire by gratifying it with the objects of desire. Such gratification ends in weariness; such gratification ends in satiety; and the Self, which is greater than all objects of desire, will sting the Soul still onward to seek a deeper satisfaction.

After a time the man on the Path of Karma discovers this. He finds he is weary, dissatisfied, and discontented: that the more he acquires, the more causes of discontentment arise around him, and deep and bitter is his disappointment. Then reaction comes. He sees that here there is no satisfaction, no gratification. He says: "Let me fly from the world, let me renounce all objects of the senses, for here on the Path of Karma there is neither peace nor contentment to be found"; and out of sheer disgust the man will for a time rush away from all the objects of the senses, and seek to find peace in the solitude of recluse life. But, to his disappointment, to his discouragement, to his grief, he discovers that not by fleeing from the objects of desire can desire itself be extinguished. He finds that the taste for them pursues him even into the jungle. The images of the sense objects come after him to his cave and hermitage, and the man dwells mentally upon such images of the senses; although the body is held back, the man is still a prey to desires, he is still torn by the contending passions of his lower nature. For desire is not extinguished by external withdrawal from the objects of desire. Its roots are deeper in human nature, and the Path of Karma must be further trodden if desire is to disappear.

Then there comes to him the Voice of the Lord in the silence of this inactivity that he has forced upon himself. The Voice will come through the silence, and it speaks the words of eternal wisdom: "Man winneth not freedom from action by abstaining from activity, nor by mere renunciation (of activity) doth he rise to perfection." * Not with outer inactivity, but with freedom from desire, is this Path of Karma to be trodden. Freedom from action will not be won by the bodily abstention from activity. The path of action must yet be trodden before the soul may be free. The freedom is won on that path itself by learning a deeper lesson than the removal of the body from the city to the jungle. He learns that lesson from the same divine source, the duty of the man living in the world who yet would be free from attachment. He learns that he must act, but that the motive must be changed. He must tread the path of action, but the motive is to be new and divine in its character. And that same Voice, the same great Teacher, breathes once more its lesson into the soul of the weary and exhausted seeker for freedom: "As the ignorant act from attachment to action, O Bhârata, so the wise act without attachment, desiring the maintenance of mankind." †

Here is a change indeed. Not to rush away into outer inactivity, deserting the place which his karma had marked out in the world; not to desert the duty to his family or to his nation; but to bring into the discharge of those duties a new spirit, carrying on his action inspired by a new

* *Bhagavad Gîtâ*, iii. 4. † *Bhagavad Gîtâ*, iii. 25.

motive. His place may be that of a man whose duty it is to acquire wealth. Let him acquire it, but, where the ignorant would acquire wealth in order to enjoy the fruit, let him work without attachment; let the wealth flow into his hands, but let him take it as a steward for the world, and not as its possessor. He works for the benefit of mankind, and not from attachment to action. Such a man will turn his wealth into new lines of active work for man. He will plan magnificent schemes; he will think and work and toil for the benefit of man. As others work and toil for the benefit of their own personal selves and their immediate family, he will work for others, and thus use his powers for the benefit of mankind.

Here a subtler temptation attacks him. This work for the maintenance of mankind even may have a personal object running through it, and may start from a subtler root of action, may have a different kind of looking for result. For a man who plans out great schemes of benevolence is anxious that the schemes should succeed. He wants success, and part of his motive is this longing for success, and for the gratification of seeing the fruits of his labours. Or perhaps it may be that he desires the love and gratitude of his fellow-men, and to gain their approbation. Thus a personal return for his action may be sought. But that must not be. If any personal motive comes in he is bound by the fruit of his action, he is fettered by the desired result.

And so the same Lord who before had taught him, the same Divine Teacher who had made him understand that freedom from outer activity was not freedom from action, that the wise man must act for the sake of serving mankind, now gives him a deeper lesson, now carries him on to a still further step on the path—it is the grand lesson of renouncing every fruit of action, the loving, joyful surrender of every motive which has its roots in the personal self. The lesson comes in those words of the Lord: "Thy business is with the action only, never with its fruits," even though the fruits be the love and gratitude that give delight to the lower man. "Never with its fruits"—that must not mingle with the motive. And then the Teacher goes on to say: "Let not the fruit of action be thy motive, nor be thou to inaction attached." *

Perfect renunciation. No longer moved by personal desire to enjoy the fruit here; no longer by the personal desire to enjoy the fruit on the other side of death; no longer by the higher personal desire to reap the love and gratitude of his fellowmen; but the renunciation of all desires, the doing of action with no regard to the fruit. Let success come; what is it to the doer? Let failure come; what matters it to him who has done his work?

* *Bhagavad Gîtâ*, ii. 47.

"Balanced evenly in success and failure: equilibrium is called Yoga."* Equal in success and failure, in pleasure and pain, honour and dishonour, in love and in hatred. No motive that touches the lower self is mingled with the activity. The action is the work of the Lord, and, whatever the result, it accrues to the Lord. Plan and scheme for the benefit of man, and your scheme fails. It is well. Plan and scheme for the benefit of man, and your scheme succeeds. It is well. Success was not the object; failure was not the object. The only object was the performance of duty. Whatever the fruit of the action, the man remains untouched and undisturbed. Action is his duty. This is the true treading of the Path of Karma —not seeking action when it is not present, nor refusing to perform it when it is there. Willing to work, if work be duty; willing to be inactive, if no work comes within the duty of the moment—absolute indifference to every result. The man who is thus treading the Path of Karma may be living in a palace, may be fed with the most delicate and savoury dishes, all around him may lie objects of gratification to the senses; he remains unaffected. Let them come, let them go, "the senses move among the objects of sense,"† the "I" remains untouched and undisturbed. They give him no gratification; they give him no repulsion.

* *Bhagavad Gîtâ*, ii. 48. † *Bhagavad Gîtâ*, v. 9.

He neither repulses objects when they are present, nor desires them when they are absent. He is hurled from a palace to a hovel; instead of rich clothes he is clad in rags; instead of savoury dishes he has to live on broken food that may be given him by the poor—what matters it to him? He desired not what has passed away, any more than he rejected it when it was present. He is as happy in the hovel as in the palace, as happy in the palace as in the hovel. Neither attracts him, neither repels him. They are outer energies of Nature, passing illusions of Matter. What are they to him who has attained renunciation, and cares nothing for fruit, but only for the doing of duty? A sublime life, a noble life, one of the hardest of all lives to live—to live surrounded by every object, and absolutely indifferent to all,—to move through riches or poverty, through pleasure or pain, through honour or ignominy, with equal contentment, with equal serenity, and with equal calm. To what a height has such a man risen as he treads the difficult Path of Karma, now become the Path of Karma Yoga! He is approaching the stage of Yoga where all Paths blend into one, and where the Supreme will unveil Himself to the man who is free from the illusions of matter.

Out of this life—the life that asks nothing, that seeks nothing, that claims nothing, that refuses nothing—out of that life wisdom arises. How can the eyes remain without discrimination of him who has learned to discriminate between the outer activities and the Self by the renunciation of desire while performing the action? Such a man becomes wise by action as another may become wise by intellectual study and contemplation. But there is another Path—the Path of Bhakti—and that must blend with both the others when the journey is complete.

Then a glimpse of the Supreme is gained. The eyes, purged of all desires, perceive Him under all veils of matter. The heart, purified from all desires, sees deep within itself the one Self of all. Then from that sight of the Supreme, from that glimpse of the eternal Beauty, the last touch is put to Karma Yoga, the last step is taken on the karmic Path, and that is the lesson of sacrifice. It still comes from the same Teacher, and is poured out from the same Divine lips; once more to the soul that is purified, that has learned the lesson of activity as duty, the lesson of renunciation of fruit, and that is working out the law, comes the final, the supreme, lesson:—"The world is bound by all action unless performed with sacrifice for object." * Every action now is to be done, not only without desire for its fruit, but with the object of sacrifice to the Supreme. Man has to become a co-worker with the Lord, a fellow-worker with the Deity

* *Bhagavad Gîtâ*, iii. 9.

Himself. Once he did action with fruit as motive. Then he learned to do it for mankind. Then he learned to do it for duty's sake, renouncing every fruit, taking everything as the same. Lastly he learns to do it with sacrifice as object, and every action becomes an act of worship, every action is an act of homage to the Supreme. Then, indeed, on the Path of Karma he tastes the joy of the Lord; then there begins to flow into him the bliss of the Self. He learns to renounce and to stand without attachment to the lower, and the higher flows in and fills his being and he knows himself as one with the Supreme. The deepest joy suffuses the whole of his nature; work is done as sacrifice, and the joy of the sacrificer is his. He shares in the life of Îshwara, he is a channel for the working of the Lord, he sees all action done as sacrifice to Him—He the only Worker, the one Sacrifice; He the Giver, and He the Taker of the fruit and the Enjoyer, the whole bound up in Him. And when that perfect sacrifice is accomplished, when the life gives always and takes from none save God, when the light flows out through it, but it asks nothing for itself, when the sun shines on the uttermost limits of the world and cares nothing for its own radiance and claims nothing save to belong to the Lord—then the Path of Karma passes into the Supreme Peace. Then man has found his goal, he reaches union with the Self.

So may we close with the teaching and the promise of the same Divine Instructor, whose precepts we have been striving to understand and to apply to our own lives, the teaching and the promise embodied in the mighty words: "The disciplined self, moving among sense objects with senses free from attraction and repulsion, mastered by the Self, goeth to Peace . . . . This is the Brahman state, O son of Prithâ. Having attained thereto, none is bewildered. Who, even at the death-hour, is established therein, he goeth to the Nirvâna of Brahman." *

* *Bhagavad Gîtâ*, ii. 64, 72.

GNYÂNA MÂRGA

WE were considering yesterday the way in which the Self might be sought by way of activity. We were studying that Path of action which so many of mankind must tread. Studying that Path, we learned how a man might gradually grow from attachment to non-attachment, how he might practise renunciation, how finally by sacrifice he might attain to the Supreme. This afternoon we are to consider the second of the great Paths lead-to the Self, that which is called the Gnyâna Mârga, or the Path of Wisdom—a Path trodden by the minority only, a Path which is not suited to the mass of mankind, a Path which is encumbered with special dangers, most particularly for the untrained, for those who have not accomplished the preliminary steps of purification. For neither about the Path of Karma, nor about the Path of Bhakti, is there the same danger of misunderstanding, the same likelihood of confusion, the same possibility of going utterly wrong, if due preparation for its higher stages has not been properly made, as there is in connection with Gnyâna Mârga. We are to trace it from its early stages to its later growth. We are to see how it leads from the life of the world to the goal of the Supreme. We shall take it stage by stage, in order that we may understand it, in order that we may avoid misconception, and may not fall into those traps which are on either side of it, and which ensnare so many unwary pilgrims.

I have said that the entrance to it is only possible to some. The way which begins in pure intellect, although it transcends pure intellect in its later stages, implies the development in the man who would tread it at all, of a wide, of a large, of a penetrating and a lofty intellect. The senses must be subjugated, the mind must be cultivated—and cultivated not with a view of obtaining anything by its exercise save the pure enjoyment of pure wisdom at a later time; it must not be tainted by desire for anything that may come as the result of knowledge, connected with the gratification of the lower nature of man. As we saw yesterday, intellect is often used to subserve the gratification of the senses. Science is often employed in order to increase the accumulation of material objects, in order to increase the comforts of the physical world. The man who is preparing to tread the Path of Wisdom must have outgrown all those lower desires, must have turned aside from the attraction of the senses, and must find, at first in knowledge and later in wisdom, the reward which is all-sufficient in itself, and which needs no adventitious advantages in order to be attractive to the inner man. Tamas must be entirely subjugated, must no longer have power to influence his nature, no longer have power to hold the feet of the man in the mire belonging to the lowest world. Rajas, the quality of activity, must be turned away from all those lines of action that have to do with material objects. Rajas must be turned in the direction of gaining knowledge; all its energies must be concentrated on the accumulation of knowledge, before the path of true wisdom can be approached at all.

In the earlier stages of the Path, what we may call the entrance stage, knowledge will be sought for its own sake. You may pick out the souls that have entered on this Path by watching how a man will gradually develop within himself, or be born with, the tendency innate in the Ego to search for knowledge, asking for nothing save the delight of discovery, save the joy of a wide intellect, of the conscious increase of powers of the mind. You will find such men scattered over the world, though few and far between—men who care nothing for fame, nothing for wealth, who are not seeking the applause of their fellows or the gratification of their lower nature. They are devotees of knowledge for the joy that knowledge gives. They find in its pursuit its own reward. They are passionate in their search after knowledge up to death. They long to know the nature of the universe, the nature of man, to plunge into the heights and depths of existence, to fathom all the secrets of Nature, to assimilate all the knowledge which the outer world can give. Knowledge, as I said, is not wisdom. Knowledge lies in the observation of facts, the observation of phenomena, in gathering those observations together, in arranging them side by side and tracing out the relation between them, in searching for some underlying principle which may group and classify and co-ordinate these separately observed phenomena, and then, in welding them together into some hypothesis which fits them all, will explain them all. Then the student takes the hypothesis based upon observation and upon reasoning by inference from the results of observation, and, comparing that hypothesis anew with the phenomena of the outer world, he devises experiments to test it, seeking for all possible methods by which its accuracy or inaccuracy may be discovered; and thus having completed his experiments, he can say, "I have experimented and found an invariable result, which was foretold by the hypothesis." Then the result is regarded as a Law in Nature, on which men may build with certainty. A man of science will work in this fashion, doing admirable work of its own kind, watching carefully, observing with endless patience, showing what has been described as "the sublime patience of the investigator," and asking Nature questions time after time, month after month, year after year, until her answer is ever repeated with undeviating identity, so that he may build on a rock of truth on which Science may securely stand, and advance to fresh discoveries. If you would understand the way in which knowledge is thus gained, take as an example Charles Darwin, the great English Naturalist, whose marvellous experiments were the admiration of his own generation as well as of those that follow. You will find him, for instance, devoting himself to the cultivation of certain plants, changing the soil, regulating the light, observing all the conditions that surrounded them, giving to one more, to another less, varying the conditions in every possible way, and noting down the results of each variation; then, perhaps, repeating the observations a hundred times over. Doing this, that no inaccuracy might creep in, that no hasty inference might be made, that no partial view should be taken as the whole, that no blunder should be made in tracing the thread of causation, and that mere succession of phenomena should not mislead the inquirer into a mistaken view of a sequence which was never changed. This is admirable in its devotion to truth, in its candour, determining to give endless labour before an assertion is made. All this is real worship of that God of truth whose hand is shown in the laws of the physical world. And this very patience is the proof of the real and unadulterated desire for knowledge which animates the man. To such a worker nothing in Nature is small and nothing is great. Every phenomenon is observed with the same patient accuracy, whether it be the course of suns or the movement of small microscopic creatures in a drop of water. Who can tell where knowledge may be hidden, who can say where the finger of Nature is pointing to a new discovery? It may be that the movements of a particle observed under the microscope may be more significant of the Divine working in Nature than the course of a comet in its orbit as it whirls through space and plunges into the infinite depths. Nothing is either small or great; everything is the manifestation of Nature, and may hide the secret of the working. He learns, as he studies, that Nature works as carefully, as exquisitely, as delicately, with the same geometrical accuracy and precision of form, when she fashions the shell of an invisible diatom, as when she makes a solar system of planets revolving round their central sun. And this view of Nature—that all in Nature is equally worthy of observation—is interwoven into the very life of the man who gives himself to knowledge and follows her to her obscurest corners. Shall I tell you a curious fable which presents this truth in a forcible way by a striking picture, which really expresses as well as anything I have ever read this characteristic of the searcher after knowledge which is marked in the earlier stages of this Path?

A great Russian writer of fiction, that some of you may have read, Tourguenieff, gives the following fable to illustrate the way in which Nature works over her minutest products as over her greatest and grandest creations. He says that he travelled through a mighty rock-hewn temple—a vast temple whose limits were invisible, lost in obscurity on either side, so vast that only the darkness seemed to bound it, and the living rock was above it and below it, and the living rock made its pillars and the arches of its gigantic roof. As he went through that wonderful temple, he saw sitting in it a mighty Goddess, gigantic in her figure, magnificent in her form, her face radiant with Divine power, love, and intellect. Strength and wisdom were incarnate in this heroic figure, seated lonely amid the immensity of the rock-hewn fane. She was engaged at work—bending over her task in intensest contemplation, her fingers busily employed in shaping some object, in producing some creature. Her mighty brows were bent above it in rapt attention; all her thought was given to her labour. Silence was around her, silence on every side. He approached in fear, and thought, "Surely this Goddess is fashioning the brain of some mighty hero or of some great thinker; some great one of mankind is occupying her attention, and all her powers are bent to the gigantic work." He approached in reverence and asked her what she wrought. She raised her face and said—and her deep soft voice reverberated through the space around her—"I fashion the hind-leg of a flea."

Such is the fable. The meaning is clear enough: In it is depicted the spirit that votaries of knowledge learn when they meet the mighty Goddess, that for Her everything is worthy of perfection. The smallest and the greatest, the tiniest and the mightiest alike, have got in them something of the Nature-Spirit, and students search into the secrets of Nature with eager and reverent minds, and thus knowledge increases, and science after science is builded.

The microscope unfolds the infinite world of the minute, and the telescope unveils the infinite world of the vast. Above and below, in all the six directions of space, new fields stretch out for ever new discoveries. New knowledge beckons the student from every side. World after world is there to be studied in our solar system ; world after world to be conquered. Let us suppose that a man is equipped, as a man may be, to study all the regions of solar space, that he is held by no limits of physical existence. Let the man who seeks Knowledge pass from the physical to the astral world, invisible to fleshly eyes to-day. He has to acquire there the knowledge of a variety of objects, of a diversity of phenomena, and of new possibilities. As the intellect evolves new capacities, new depths of being unfold before the dazzled eyes. He conquers the astral ; other worlds unfold before him, the world of intellect—a new infinity of things to be observed, a new infinity and diversity of experiences to be gained. Let us say that he has conquered the physical, astral, and mental regions. He has only conquered the three worlds of this tiny sphere ; and the rest of the infinite universe stretches around him, unknown, unexplored. Suppose that he conquers planet after planet until every one of them is as familiar to him with its wide field of phenomena as our city is to ourselves. Imagine that, after the conquest of this solar sytem, he starts to conquer other systems through all the infinity of space. Where shall knowledge find its terminus ? Where shall the intellect acknowledge itself exhausted ? Knowledge piled on knowledge, worlds heaped over worlds, systems massed upon systems, and still the unknown stretches around him on every side, and still the unexplored beckons him to its mysterious distances, and the longing for knowledge spurs on the lagging soul. There is a story of the pillar of fire in which Mahâdeva stretched upwards and downwards, lost in the infinities of space; and Brahmâ soared upwards a thousand years and found that it still towered beyond Him, and Vishnu plunged downwards for a thousand years, and the fire still stretched below Him. That might be taken as the picture of the Infinite Divine Being who manifests Himself in all the worlds, and in all those worlds only a fraction of His possibilities are shown. There is no end to Aparâ Vidyâ, to the knowledge of phenomena; there is no end to seeking. The soul's pinions flag in the unceasing depths of space, and wearied out the mind falls back defeated, baffled, unable to complete its knowledge.

But during the search for knowledge, during the gathering of observations, the Self has been speaking to the heart of man. The Self has been whispering that It is hidden beneath the veil of Mâyâ, that these objects are but illusory, and that the eternal and endless are but one. That it is not necessary to acquire all knowledge before true wisdom may be gained; that it is not necessary to pervade the universe before the Self may be discriminated under the veil of illusion, and the step which leads from knowledge to wisdom may be made at any point of the search, for the Self is hidden everywhere: "nor is there aught, moving or unmoving, that may exist bereft of Me."* Dimly the man senses the One beneath the many. Dimly he senses the Self under the veils that hide It from the eyes of men. Weary of a search that is endless, for objects had followed upon objects; weary of a Path that has no goal, for observation of phenomena is endless for the intellect, the man dimly at first, but still truly, knows that he must leave the objects, must leave observation, must leave the outer world, must turn inward and not outward, that he must look at the centre and not at the circumference of the circle. Nowhere on the surface, though he search the universe, shall he find the Self; everywhere, if he look inwards, shall the Self be manifest. Then there awakens in that man, slowly and gradually asserting itself, making itself felt in all this turmoil of phenomena, what is called Viveka, discrimination —the discrimination of the Eternal amid the transient, of the Self within the objects, of the One concealed in the many, of the true end of all seeking, the Infinite, the Eternal Sat. He begins to discriminate between the show and the substance, between the illusory and the real, between the false and the truth that underlies it. This quality of discrimination is the first step out of mere know-

* *Bhagavad Gîtâ*, x. 39.

ledge into true wisdom. The man discriminates the Eternal from the transitory, and his foot is placed on the higher stage of the Path. The result of the growth of the quality of discrimination within him is the feeling of Vairâgya, the disgust of the outer appearances—a feeling of shrinking away from them, a desire to fly from them, a longing to escape from them anywhere out of the sight of man, into silence, into solitude, away from the family life into the silence, at least, of Nature. But even there phenomena are to be sensed, and the Self is still hidden under illusion. He has been tricked by this beautiful show; like a foolish child he has been deluded into thinking that the toy he plays with is a living thing, that the doll has life and can answer back to his speech, can experience as he experiences. He is almost angry with the outer world, that had held him bound in threads that seemed links of iron, but in reality are mere webs of gossamer made of glamour and unreality.

Out of that disgust which follows on the glimpses given by true discrimination, he is lifted by the knowledge that progress is possible for him, and that there are six mental attributes which he must acquire, to some extent at least, ere he can find the Self amidst its hidden coverings, ere he can truly recognise the Self beneath the veils that enshroud it. The worst enemy of man is himself, in the lowest nature that answers to the physical and astral worlds. The man must learn dispassion by the study of experiences, by disillusionment, until he has developed certain powers, without which the later stages of the Path may not be trodden, although they may be talked about and discussed by the intellect alone. He must acquire control of the mind, control of the body, so that neither body nor mind may have the slightest power to disturb him, and so that they will never move merely in answer to impulses from without. He must develop that wide breadth of view which understands and tolerates all, which realises the one aim under the many methods, which can see the same object being sought by a great diversity of ways. He must develop that endurance without which search for the Self will fail—that endurance which makes the soul strong. No soul that is weak can find the Self by the way of Wisdom. He must develop confidence in his own divinity, he must feel himself Divine and know that therefore everything is possible to him, and he must develop that balance which nothing can disturb. For how shall the Self become visible if there be want of balance, preventing clearness and distinctness of vision?

When he has developed all these qualities, then it is said that he is ready to enter on the Path that leads to liberation, ready to stand as a candidate before the gate which, opening, shall give to his tread the Path of pure Wisdom for which he has trained himself by all the past experiences, by the purity of his developed intellect, the keenness of his developed mind, by the reason that he has sharpened in his struggle, and by the acquiring of all those other qualities with which he has crowned his intellectual life. Then, and not till then, he is said to be an Adhîkârî, the man who is ready for the final teaching, the wisdom concerning the Self.

What is that Wisdom? That wisdom is the immediate knowledge of the Self—the knowledge of the One, the Infinite, the Eternal, the seeing of That everywhere, through every veil recognising It, and identifying the one Self wherever It appears, and It is everywhere. Wisdom is defined by Shrî Krishna Himself, who has traced the Path of Wisdom as well as the Path of Action and the Path of Devotion, and has summed up into a single sentence the true wisdom, that which is meant by the word Gnyâna. He declared: "I, O Gudâkesha, am the Self seated in the heart of all beings; I am the beginning, the middle, and also the end of all beings."* And then later he declared in detail what was wisdom: "Humility, unpretentiousness, harmlessness, forgiveness, rectitude, service of the teacher, purity, steadfastness, self-control, indifference to the objects of the senses, and also absence of egoism, insight into the pain and evil of birth, death, old age and sickness,

* *Bhagavad Gîtâ*, x. 20.

unattachment, absence of self-identification with son, wife or home, and constant balance of mind in wished-for and unwished-for events, unflinching devotion to Me, without union with another, resort to sequestered places, absence of enjoyment in the company of men, constancy in the Adhyâtmâ wisdom, understanding of the object of essential wisdom : that is declared to be wisdom ; all against it is ignorance. That, the Light of all lights, is said to be beyond darkness ; wisdom, the object of wisdom, the end of wisdom, seated in the hearts of all." * That is wisdom as declared by the lips of the Lord of Wisdom, and when He was speaking of the man constant and unceasing in his pursuit of that wisdom, He spake of the Adhikârî, and defined wisdom as the knowledge of the essential Nature of Brahman.† Nothing less than that is Wisdom. Everything except that is ignorance. Knowledge is ignorance, if it know only the outer effects. Science is ignorance if it be concerned only with the Mâyâ of phenomena. Wisdom resides alone in the knowledge of the Self in His essential Nature, His all - pervading identity.

Let us follow, however poorly, some of the alphabet of this knowledge of the Self which is Wisdom. The Self is One. Variety is of the outer universe,

* *Bhagavad Gîtâ*, xiii. 7-11, 17.

† Compare *Bhagavad Gîtâ*, viii. 3.

the play of illusions, the veil of Mâyâ, which blinds us to the Unity which is the only Existence, the only Life, the only Lord of the whole universe beyond whom there is nothing; and He is One. The Self is actionless. Activity is of Prakriti, the veil with which the Self surrounds Himself, the play of guṇas. The variety and activity in Nature are the outer semblances—the visible appearances of that Unity. The change of one thing into another, birth, maturity and death, the wheel of constant change of living objects—these are the play of the guṇas, and the guṇas revolve, whilst the Self remains unchanged. All this is the Lord surrounded by His Mâyâ, Vishnu with His Lila, the play of the universe; all is the thought of that Supreme. The forms are changing and therefore illusory; the life is Himself and He is all. It is said that "He who seeth that Prakriti verily performeth all actions, and that the Self is actionless, he seeth." * This is the working out of discrimination, the clear vision between the Self and all those veils of Nature which enshroud and hide Him. The Self is actionless. His apparent movements belong to external Nature. The Self is everywhere, seated in all, beyond all. Once more the words of wisdom come forth: "Seeing indeed everywhere the same Îshvara equally dwelling." †

* *Bhagavad Gîtâ*, xiii. 29. † *Bhagavad Gîtâ*, xiii. 28.

How hard the lesson to learn! Equally dwelling everywhere, in the lowest and the vilest as well as in the loftiest and the greatest, in the atom of the dust as well as in the central sun of the universe, in all that is vile and base, the Self of the profligate the same as the Self of the saint! What lesson is this that the Lord is teaching? What meaning in words like these? It means that Îshvara is the same in all, for all the Universe is His own manifestation, and doth He not say: "I am the gambling of the cheat, and the splendour of splendid things, I!"* Can you catch glimpses of that lesson? Can you understand what that means for the universe? It implies that there is need of every experience, in order that Wisdom may be perfected. If you can see the one Self in the beautiful, the noble, and the sublime, can you also see Him in the lowly, the ignoble, and the repulsive? To a man who can thus see, there is nothing ugly and nothing beautiful—all are parts of Himself, necessary for the present evolution. Everything has its own place, everything its own position, playing its own part and gathering experience; for He is infinite, and endless must be the variety that shall show forth even a fragment of Himself. You see the differences, and therefore you see imperfection; you see a fragment and not the whole of which it is a part. It is as if you took a

* *Bhagavad Gîtâ*, x. 36.

weaver's carpet, and saw the reverse side where the threads end, and saw not the pattern; nor do you see the upper side, where black is wanted as well as the exquisite shades of lovely glow, all falling into their rightful places. That one Self is in everyone, and not one is outside His life. No fragment is excluded from the whole. Our purblind eyes see only the imperfection, they see not the Self working towards perfection; the whole is evolving to a perfect Nature, and the most hideous is on the way to Divine beauty, the most simple is on the way to Divine intelligence. Therefore see Him everywhere, seated equally in all, and then you will have true discrimination, and the Self shall shine forth undimmed.

Another lesson has still to be learned: all that exists and attracts, everything that has in it something of the element of attraction, has it only because of the Self. Were it possible that the Self should not be there, all attractiveness would vanish. Do you remember how Maitreyî prayed her husband to teach her the lesson of immortality, and he answered:—"Behold, not indeed for the husband's sake the husband is dear, but for sake of the Self is dear the husband. Behold, not indeed for the wife's sake the wife is dear, but for the sake of the Self is dear the wife. Behold, not for the sons' sake the sons are dear, but for the sake of the Self are dear the sons. Behold, not for the property's sake property is dear, but for the sake of the Self is dear the property." Nay, not even "for the Gods' sake the Gods are dear, but for the sake of the Self are dear the Gods."* Thus the mighty Sage explained to his listening wife the mystery of the Self, and the mystery of the love that goes out from each to the other separated being. This love is the Self seeking Himself in another. So the Sage gave many another illustration, teaching how everything is dear for the Self within it and not for the veil of illusion that surrounds it. "The Self is verily to be seen, to be heard, to be meditated upon." That is the secret of immortality. Such was the teaching of the Sage to the wife he loved; such the words of the teacher speaking to the listening soul of the disciple, and unveiling the secret of wisdom. When this lesson is learned, "Thou art That"; when this lesson is acquired, "I am He," there is no difference. That is the position of the true Gnyânî, of the liberated soul who cannot any longer be affected by the play of the guṇas, by the revolving wheel of Nature from which he has escaped. There is One, there is none other. That lesson, really learned, is the breaking of every bond, the liberation of the soul. In such a man all desires are dead, the activities of the mind are at rest. He doeth nothing,

* *Brihadâranyakopanishad*, IV. v. 6.

because the Self doeth all through him. There is the secret of "action in inaction," there is the secret of true Wisdom. He may act with the body, with the mind, but *he* is doing nothing.

How then does he live? Ere saying another word about that, let me remind you of a striking story that you may distinguish between the true wisdom and the lip wisdom. It is told in one of the sacred books, the story of Shrî Krishna and the Gopis, in relation to the Great Rishi Durvâsa. For some time that Rishi ate but once in the year, and then required for his single meal an enormous amount of food. The Gopis were wont to carry him this yearly repast; when the time came to carry the food, they gathered much rich food and piled it on many a platter, and a number of them started heavily laden with these delicate dishes. They came near his âshrama, and a river rolled broad between them and the abode of the saint, and they could not cross over the tossing waters; they feared the anger of Durvâsa, and they went back to their Lord, and said: "What shall we do? There is the stream which we cannot cross, and if the Rishi's wrath burst forth, the worlds will be burned up." The Lord smiled and said: "Go to the river and speak to it in My name, and say to that river, 'If Krishna be a Brahmachâri, roll back and let us pass.'" And they said, "What is this that we are to say? Krishna surrounded with his Gopis, and still a celibate?" But knowing that the Lord was wise, they, going to the river, spake those words of power, and the waters heard their voice and rolled to either side, making liquid walls, and the Gopis trod on dry ground and reached the abode of the saint and carried the food to him. He emptied platter after platter and finished the food. When the time came for the Gopis to go back, the river again was running high, and once more they said, "How shall we cross the river?" And they went to the Sage for help, and the Sage said: "Go to the river and say, 'If Durvâsa be but an eater of air, then roll back and let us pass.'" The Gopis said to themselves, "Behold, he has eaten all this food, and nothing is left, and we are to say that he lives upon air!" But there was nothing else to do, and going to the river they spake again the words of power: "If Durvâsa be an eater of air only, then roll back and let us pass." And again the waters heard the words and rolled back and made a path for their feet to tread. Then they related to the Lord the facts and asked Him to explain. And He taught them the lesson that the man of perfect Wisdom is unaffected by action, unchanged by all that surrounds him. The true Gnyânî is unaffected by action, he cannot be touched by the phenomena of the outer world.

But here a mistake often comes in. Men who are

only wise by lips but not in reality, who repeat phrases but have not developed the true life of the Self, who say "I am Brahman," but are affected by everything, who are not disciplined and dispassionate, who seek the gratification of the senses, and then say, "It is only the body that seeks it, I am unaffected"—those men are deluded, and unconsciously, or even consciously, hypocritical; for they know not that the true Gnyânî uses the guṇas, but is not used by them; he uses them to carry out the purpose of the universe, but is not swayed by them, and never can be affected by them. The man who cannot resist the temptations of the body, and who then says, "It is only the body that acts, I am Brahman"—such a one is but a man of lip-phrases and possesses not the real wisdom, and is affected and degraded by his vice. The wise man can take up any activity, can use it for the purpose of the Lord, and is but a channel for the maintenance of the world. He is moved from within and not from without. As a master he moves to his toil, and not as a slave is driven to his labour. He is free and not a bondsman. To tread the Path in words, being mastered by the body whilst speaking the words of wisdom, is to fall a prey to delusion, and to delay the progress of the soul. To that base end the labours of the great teachers have been turned, and the Vedânta has been used as an excuse for vile living; the pretence of dispassion has been set up where the reality is not. It was to avoid this danger that in the old days none might learn those lessons save he who had the qualifications. He whose desires were dead, whose passions were conquered, who had experienced disgust of the world—that man only was the fitted pupil, and to him only the Guru taught the Mysteries.

Such, then, is the Path of Wisdom, and such are some of the difficulties of its treading. So may man escape from the world and pass into a life of freedom.

It may be well for you, however, to remember that if this escape be sought for the separated Self and not for the service of the universe, then, though the liberation may last for countless ages, the man will have ultimately to return in order to gain the uttermost perfection. For it is written in the sacred Upanishad that not by knowledge alone the Self is found, but by knowledge wedded to devotion.* Liberation may be gained by pure wisdom, and the soul passes into and abides in Janarloka, freed from birth and deaths; but that perfect life, which asks for nothing, which is content to be in bondage while the Lord is manifest, while Îshwara is working, that means the blending of Wisdom with Devotion, and thereby only is perfection gained.

* *Mundakopanishad*, III. ii. 4.

BHAKTI MÂRGA

"THEY who with Manas fixed on Me, ever harmonised worship Me, with faith supreme endowed, these, in My opinion," said Shrî Krishna, "are best in Yoga." And then He went on to say that "The difficulty of those whose minds are set on the Unmanifested is greater; for the path of the Unmanifested is hard for the embodied to reach. Those verily who, renouncing actions in Me, and intent on Me, worship meditating on Me, with whole-hearted Yoga, these I speedily lift up from the ocean of death and existence, O Pârtha, their minds being fixed on Me." * Those are the words in which the great Lord of Yoga instructed His beloved disciple. The fixing of the mind on Îshvara, the revealed Lord, the worship intent ever upon Him, the constant meditation fixed upon the one object, those who thus act, He said, are speedily raised up by Him from this ocean into which souls are plunged, life after life, and from which, wearied as it were, they long to escape. This devotion, which he thus

* *Bhagavad Gîtâ*, xii. 2, 5–7.

described, this fixing of the mind, this constant meditation, this earnest worship, these are summed up in the word Bhakti or Love; and it is the Path of Love, the Bhakti Mârga, which we are to study at this our concluding meeting.

There is one wide difference between the Path of Wisdom and the Path of Love, which stands out before our eyes clear and distinct from beginning to end; and this difference is in what we may call the object of the devotee and the object of the Gnyânî; these are distinct, the one from the other, in a sense—although, of course, fundamentally and essentially they are one and the same. The distinction is alluded to in the shloka that I have quoted, as to the difficulty of treading and reaching the Path of the Unmanifested. He who treads the Path of Wisdom, the Gnyânî, seeks the Self, the One Existence, the Infinite, the Eternal, and the Unmanifested, underlying and pervading all, supporting all, and hidden beneath all. But as we saw in our study yesterday, it is by discrimination, by wisdom, that he reaches this knowledge of the Self, and its supreme expression is the "So'ham"—"I am He"—the perfect identity with the One without a second. But when we look at the object to which the Bhakta directs his attention, his love, his worship, his undeviating faith, we find that this object is the supreme Îshvara, the embodied Lord, the manifested God, the one Lord making Himself manifest in form, and so becoming a concrete object of love and adoration. In fact, where Bhakti is to be aroused, it must be directed towards a Being who shows what, in the widest sense of the term, may be said to be the limits of individuality. However much we may extend our conception of individuality, casting aside all by which it is limited when we are dealing with an individual who is human, it ends after all in the very fundamental idea of limitation; the Lord of the Universe, Îshvara, the Supreme, has imposed a self-limitation for the purpose of manifestation, in order that the universe may be; and this Lord of the Universe is the object towards which the aspirations, the love, the worship of all beings in the universe may be directed.

We find still further that this Supreme Îshvara who would be called in the western term the "Personal God"—although the word "personal" brings in an element that we must necessarily exclude in our thought—this Supreme Îshvara still further manifests Himself from time to time, by way of Avatâras, in order to give man, as it were, a still more concrete embodiment, to which his love may turn and his adoration may be addressed, a still more clear individuality which may awaken his heart, which may attract his emotion, towards whom worship may be directed, and to whom homage may be paid. We find in the Hindu faith, and in other faiths as well, that the Supreme manifests Himself not only as the Lord of the universe, but also in the form of man, and that in that human form He specially arouses devotion, worship, love; presenting all the attractiveness which pleases the human heart, all the beauty which captivates the human imagination. In condescension to the weakness of His creatures, in compassion for the feebleness of their thought, He comes, as it were, within the reach of their limited intelligence, within the reach of their half-blind love, and presents Himself as an Avatâra, manifesting in human form some of the perfections of the Supreme.

In studying human faiths, in studying the religions of the world, we find that this is well-nigh universal, and that a divine-human Form occupies the central altar of worship; and although beyond Him the Higher is recognised, nay, although even beyond Îshvara Himself the One without a second is dimly seen, the human heart clings to the feet of the manifested Lord, and the human emotions find their rest and their home in Him. Whether it be under the sacred name of Râmachandra or Shrî Krishna, whether it be under the name of the Christ or the name of the Buddha, you will find that humanity specially craves to worship a Being, and seeks in devotional emotion that satisfaction which no abstract conception of infinity can afford. To those who tread the Path of Bhakti this object of worship must be the goal of the Path. For how can man, in the fullest sense of the word, feel the ecstasy of love towards the conception of a boundless Existence, of limitless space; and how without those limitations that make an object "real" to us, shall the human heart be able to find its rest in God?

So it is then that along this Path of Love we always find the Bhakta seeking for his Lord. What is this love that inspires him? What is this devotion that animates him? What is this which so fully penetrates his being, and thrills through every fibre of his life, that to him there seems to be nothing true beyond the one beloved Presence, and everything else becomes dim in the light of the all-supreme Lord? He who is the very embodiment of devotion, that mighty Sage and Bhakta Nârada, has left to us teachings on Love, and therein he has described its nature, has given to us the marks, as it were, by which it may be recognised, has told us what to seek and what to find, if we would cultivate the quality of devotion.

Nârada begins by saying that the nature of Bhakti is "extreme devotion to some one";* the element of devotion to an individual is of its very nature. Later on in the same Sûtra he gives a number of definitions of this Love, giving his own last, full of that devotion which is his main, his

* *Nârada Sûtra*, translated by E. T. Sturdy, p. 19.

most striking characteristic. Definitions of Love are given according to the opinion of Vyâsa, Gârga, and Sândilya, and then Nârada says: "It is surrendering all actions to God, and feeling the greatest misery in forgetting God." * There speaks out the spirit of the true Bhakta—all the life surrendered to the object of devotion, the worst misery forgetting Him. If the heart be blinded by the veil of some other object, if some cloud arises between the soul and its Lord, and even for a moment it forgets its God, then the bitterest agony is its portion, its greatest misery—the forgetting its Lord. Thus has Nârada taught, and this is known to the heart of everyone who is blessed with a striving after devotion. Then he describes the man who has obtained this love: "Obtaining which man becomes perfect, becomes immortal, becomes satisfied; and obtaining which he desires nothing, grieves not, hates not, does not delight (in sensuous objects), makes no effort (for selfish ends); knowing which he becomes intoxicated (with joy), transfixed, and rejoices in the Self." Further, "It cannot be made to fulfil desires, for its nature is renunciation." †

That then is Bhakti, as drawn by one who is the very embodiment of it. How should such devotion be attained? Of what steps is the Bhakti Mârga composed? How shall men whose hearts are filled

* *Nârada Sûtra*, p. 28. † *Nârada Sûtra*, pp. 22, 24.

with lower loves find the Love that is supreme? How shall men whose minds run out after the objects of sense know the One, whom knowing all is known? How shall man, wrapped round with illusion, entangled with baser affections, his feet clinging to the mire of earth, how shall he attain to the love of Nârada? How shall he become the perfected Bhakta, the devotee without flaw or stain?

We must trace the early steps of this Path, as we traced the earlier steps of the others. It is almost useless to give the perfect picture, and not to trace the course of its development from the imperfect, so that one may strive from imperfection to reach perfection. We may be fascinated by the beauty of the perfection of devotion, dazzled by the splendour of a love without a flaw. But we want to learn how such love may grow in us, with what fuel to feed the fire of devotion that we may become its very flame and naught else.

Human love may serve to give us at first a faint reflection of love for the Divine. By looking on that we may learn some signs which would characterise the real Bhakta. The object would be changed, but the essential would remain the same. Think for a moment of the strongest, purest, noblest, intensest love that you have ever felt for a human being. Analyse your life deeply, and see how it was affected by that love. See how all other things become less attractive under its light. Perhaps you cared for wealth, perhaps you were devoted to literature, or perhaps you were eager in your desire for knowledge. But there shone on the horizon of your life a face which attracted you with the intensest love of your nature, which drew you in spite of yourself towards it. All the attitude of your mind was suddenly changed under the glory and the beauty of this presence. Wealth seemed to be worthless as compared with the treasure of his love. Literature seemed to be dull and wearisome as compared with the delight of conversation with him. All knowledge seemed as a withered leaf compared with the ecstasy of his embrace. Your highest delight was to be near him; your innermost being was suffused with the love of him. All other attractions weakened their power over you; all other colours grew faint beside the radiance of this bright hue. He was to you not only a friend, but teacher, guide, lover, summing up in himself many of the noblest qualities possible in man. How love for him transformed all your life! Everything took new colours in the light poured out by him. Imagine such a human love raised to the loftiest heaven; such a human love grown deeper than the profoundest ocean; imagine it enhanced by the perfection of the object of love, intensified by everything being contained in that object;

imagine that no weariness can come to it, no satiety be found in it, and you will have some faint reflection of the feeling with which the true Bhakta regards the object of his love and worship.

Swâmi Vivekânanda, speaking in America, told a somewhat graphic story in order to impress upon his hearers how very little as a rule people really longed after God. He told of a young man who came to a religious teacher and said that he wanted to find God. The sage smiled and said nothing. The young man returned time after time, ever repeating the intensity of his desire, his longing to find God. After many days the sage told him to accompany him as he went to the river to take his morning bath, and when both were in the river, the sage took hold of the young man and plunged him under the surface of the water and held him there. The young man struggled and struggled to shake off his hold. Finally he raised him out of the water and said to him, "My son, what did you long for most when under the water?" "A breath of air," gasped the youth. "Thus must the would-be disciple long after God if he would find Him. If you have this longing after God, verily He shall be found of you."

But how many have such a longing? How many really want to find God? The first thing that comes across men makes them forget the One, and the longing vanishes from their heart.

Instead of struggling for breath, the true Bhakta would have thought only of God, that he would be nearer to his goal by death under the river-stream. We want everything that comes in our way; we want wealth, honour, worldly enjoyments and possessions. How can this greedy heart of ours find room for God? As is said in the Christian story—there was no room for Mary in the inn, and our hearts are as inns which are filled with the passing travellers and have no room for the Divine guest.

None the less shall we not be without hope; and we shall see whether there is not an entrance to this Path possible. Here a great Sage has helped us—one of those great ancient Indian writers who have devoted themselves to the teaching of the higher spiritual truths—the Sage Râmânuja. He has dealt with the preliminary stages by which man develops devotion, by which he may gradually prepare himself to be a receptacle of real love.

That Sage in tracing out these preliminary steps begins at the very beginning, with the man in his body as he is living here. He first concerns himself with a man's body—how should he treat this body, how should he behave towards it? What are the necessary qualifications for the body of a man who desires the development of the characteristics of spiritual love? The first thing he speaks about is Viveka, not in the sense we used yesterday, but in a very much more elementary sense. He applies it to the discrimination of food. The man who desires that his body shall be the vehicle in which the soul penetrated by Divine love shall dwell, must have a body that is pure, and must use discrimination with regard to food. He begins with that elementary point, and says that the Bhakta must be careful in the selection of his food. He must not take that which would require suffering on the part of other sentient beings before he can enjoy it. The would-be Bhakta must not be a source of suffering and misery to others, a source of injury to creatures who are lower than himself in the scale of evolution. He must not use as food anything that possesses sentient life, as do all animal creatures. No Bhakta must touch such food. He not only pollutes the body by such food, but he degrades his soul by showing hatred instead of compassion, selfishness instead of altruism, doing injury to helpless animals instead of protecting them, doing away with the beautiful life of a harmless creature for the selfish gratification of his own palate—this is trampling on the very idea of love. Therefore, at the outset he must learn Viveka or discrimination of food. In the selection of the food that is necessary for a Bhakta, the magnetic law of purity must be followed—purity which affects the subtler bodies of man, which are liable to be polluted by outside contacts, and which should be kept clean from external pollution as well as from pollution from within. So also cleanliness should be followed that the body may in every respect be a worthy temple of the devotee who has to use it while he treads the Path of Love. He then passes on to give the great axiom, "pure food, pure mind, and constant memory of God." That is to be the law of life for the would-be Bhakta—not for him who has already attained devotion, but for one who desires to attain it.

These are the preliminary steps for finding God—for him who would arouse this divine quality of Love. The Âchârya then says that the would-be Bhakta must practise freedom from desire—his only desire must be fixed on God, his only longing must be directed to God, there must be no room for any other desire in his heart. This desire must spread out and encompass every fraction of his being, and every other desire must be driven out to make room for the one supreme attachment. Then he must practise turning his thoughts to God. This is to be a constant thing. As he tries this concentration, he will find that his mind will wander away, will go after other objects; it will wander away from the one supreme Object, and seek other things upon which to rest. But has not the Lord of Yoga said, in answer to the complaint of Arjuna, that the mind was restless as the wind and as difficult to subdue—has not He answered: "It may be curbed by constant practice."* The would-be devotee, therefore, should practise constantly to turn his mind to God. He will bring it back to the object of contemplation when it goes to other things. He will have stated times during which he will be engaged in worship, with his mind directed exclusively to the contemplation of the One.

These are only the first steps. He worships at stated times in order that presently he may worship always; he practises meditation now and again in order that presently there may be no intervals, but meditation may be ever going on, unbroken, continuous, and complete. He is only learning, so he has fixed times for worship and contemplation. He fixes his heart on the Supreme. That is not enough. That practice may lead into a life wanting in the characteristics of true Bhakti. He may find delight in his meditation, joy from contemplation, and thus may become forgetful of others and may worship for the pleasure of worshipping. But the true Bhakta does not seek to gain; he seeks to give, to give constantly, perpetually, in order that he may overcome the selfishness of human nature and eradicate the grasping tendency of the mind. Therefore the next step which is laid down is that he must

* *Bhagavad Gîtâ*, vi. 35.

do good to others. Not in contemplation is he to find his only employment; his love must flow out towards his fellow-man, and his life must be one of constant service, continual assistance, to all who are in need. He will never eradicate the grasping element unless he cultivates the giving spirit; unless he is always stripping himself in order that others may enjoy. Give, give, give, continually, for giving is of the very nature of love. Love asks for nothing save the right to give; love asks for nothing save the right to spend; love asks for no return, no gratitude. It asks for no enjoyment for itself. It asks only to be allowed to love, to spread itself out in every direction and make all happy in the embrace of the lover. As our hearts are hard and selfish even in religion itself, we have the subtlest forms of selfishness, we ruin the pure gold with the dross; therefore it is that religion, the noblest and purest of all things, sometimes becomes degraded and defiled, because men bring their selfishness into the sanctuary and convert that sacred place to a market where buying and selling goes on, so much worship for so much joy. Where there is no free giving there is no place for God.

Therefore active doing of good to others is part of the training of the devotee. How few really love, as far as their fellow-men are concerned.

We are always asking for something back, some gratification of the lower self, and we always crave and crave that something shall come from our beloved to us. That is not love, but calculation. It is a subtler form of selfishness. Pure human love pours itself out freely. It is enough to be permitted to love. The true lover does not ask more than to give his love.

Such training will more and more prepare the man to feel the true Bhakti—the love of God. Then it is said we must gain purity, and truth, and rectitude, and charity, and the absence of injury to others, and compassion. All these things are laid down as necessary on the Path, if ever we are to attain Bhakti, if ever we are to know the love that is divine. How many of these steps are we prepared to take? See these qualities wanted as preliminary steps, and then let us examine our own hearts and see where they are lacking; in beginning to supply the lack we shall be beginning to tread the Bhakti Mârga.

The company of good men is another thing that is advised. Those who are more advanced than ourselves, those who spend some of their time in conversing on subjects of a spiritual nature, or who sit together in silence meditating on the object of devotion, are the persons whose company should be sought, rather than the company of the worldly and the frivolous. Try to be with such. Man is influenced by the company into which he goes. The thoughts of other men play upon him, and he has his mind largely coloured by the atmosphere into which he goes. If he consort always with the careless and the frivolous and walk with the foolish, how shall such a man be able to gather himself in and concentrate on the Self? How shall he find his Lord? Rather let him seek a quiet life, never forgetting duty, but never seeking activity for the mere sake of distraction. Let him seek the company of the holy, and catch from them a reflection of their nobler thought and purer aspiration; for the companionship of those who love the Lord is stimulating to those who are beginning the Path.

Good books should also be read, books that stimulate devotion and set before us the noble examples of the saints and the sages of the world. Do not fritter away your time in worthless literature; do not fall into the habit of frivolous reading. You have no time to waste. When you read, read what helps you in the object of your search. If you desire to succeed in law, you will not read stories, but you will read books of jurisprudence, the history of the law of different countries; you will study their customs and eschew everything that will not help you in your search for success. Do not do less for the love of God.

When will men work for God as they work for reputation? When will they seek His face with the same ardour as they seek the toys and frivolities of earth? Teachers are not wanting; the steps are not hidden. It is the heart that is wanting, the love that is lacking, the desire which is absent. These are the things that keep us back, and not our ignorance of the way. So Nârada also taught to avoid mischievous books and vain discussions and to ponder over the Scriptures and devotional works.

Then, step by step, following these stages, treading this earlier portion, there comes a time when Îshvara, diligently sought, reverently worshipped, persistently followed though yet He was not seen, reveals Himself to His worshipper, and the Supreme is seen. Then there comes a change over the life; then a new element enters into the heart; there sweeps over the man a wave of emotion, and he is never again the same as he was before. When the Supreme has been seen, though only a glimpse of His beauty be caught, though only one gleam of that glory has come down and touched the heart of the devotee, the inner man is changed; the whole heart is revolutionised; the back is turned upon the externalities of the earth, and without effort the face is turned to God. Remember that most significant and suggestive phrase found in the Scripture of Devotion, the

Bhagavad Gîtâ, where it is said, in talking of these stages, that the objects of senses turn aside from the abstemious dweller in the body, but the flavour itself, the desire for them, the wish for them, the slightest inclination for them, turneth away when once the Supreme is seen.*

Then indeed the Path begins to shine with heavenly radiance; the first touch of the blessedness of the bliss which is the Self thrills the whole nature. How long has the Bhakta been calling to his Lord! How long has his heart been calling out for a sight of his Lord! How he has said over and over again, "How may I know Thee, O Yogî, by ceaseless meditation? In what, in what aspect art Thou to be thought of by me, O blessed Lord?"† When the Lord reveals Himself to the soul of His servant, in the radiance of that sunlight all other objects fade away—in the glory of that sight supreme, the vision of the Lord. The earth is never again the same when once that light has shone. Again clouds may arise, mistakes and feebleness may hinder the disciple's path, but he has seen, he knows, and he remembers, and has an ever-present memory to support him through every endeavour. Then it is that it is said by the Lord that such a man "having cast aside egoism, violence, arrogance, desire, wrath, covetousness, self-less and peaceful,

* *Bhagavad Gîtâ*, ii. 59. † *Bhagavad Gîtâ*, x. 17.

he is fit to become Brahman." * He is becoming fit for the constant vision of the Lord. Self-less and serene, he becomes the mirror of the Supreme Soul, and becoming Brahman, merged in Brahman, being the same to all creatures, he enters into the Lord. Such is the word of Shrî Krishna; such the promise of the Supreme.

He who has thus trained himself, who has purified his lower nature, who has become unswerving in devotion, who is serene and passionless, who does wrong to no one, who embraces all beings in the perfect love of his nature, who shuts none out from the limits of his compassion, who feels towards every creature as a mother feels for her first-born son, such a man has become fit for the presence of his Lord. He passes to the supreme abode. He is ready for the everlasting peace. For he who is love is God; he whose whole being is love is the image of the Supreme; in himself he reproduces the Divinity, for Love is God and God is Love. What can keep him then apart from that which is himself? What barrier can arise between the soul and its Lord? That soul is filled with the love of the Lord, itself is love unbounded, and as a river joining with other rivers rushes into the ocean, so does that soul that is love fly into the Ocean of love, the Supreme. The waters of the river mingle with the ocean and

* *Bhagavad Gîtâ*, xviii. 53.

become one in nature, one in quality. Who shall keep them separate? Who shall divide the soul from God? The soul knows its Lord, it bows before Him in worship, and wrapped up in the Supreme it becomes one for ever with the Lord who is Itself. And then the Lord says no longer, he shall come to Me, or he shall find Me, or he shall tread the path to My supreme abode, but He says: He verily is Myself.* He is Myself. That is the end of the Path, that the inevitable outcome of love. Love is God, and the more it is perfect the more the divine becomes manifest in it. Even in human love we see how it breaks down walls, how as we love each other we forget "I and mine" and become one. Even in our poor human love, the lover feels one with the beloved, and no longer separate. Have you not felt that all that is yours is his, and that you know no difference between yourself and him? So it is with the soul and its Lord; separated for the purposes of worship and adoration, intended to draw out the soul and all its powers, the perfected soul becomes one with its Lord—one for service, one for help, one for saving the world as He saves it, one to help the world as He helps it. In this communion between the lover and the beloved there is such utter merging and identification, that all that is done by the one is done by the other. The Bhakta becomes the

* *Bhagavad Gîtâ*, vii. 18.

Saviour of the world; he is very God, and all that God can do, he who is one with Him can also do in the creation and dissolution of the worlds.

What might not India be if she would give birth to some real Bhaktas, not those of the lips, but of the heart, of the life? If only one or two such men were found, whose hearts were so fired with Divine love that nothing was left out of its all-embracing scope, India would be saved as it were in a moment. Love would have its way. Remember you not that example of tried devotion, the boy Prahlâda? How nothing could injure him, no poison could kill, no fire could burn, no mountain could crush him, and this because he was perfectly devoted, he worshipped his Lord with all the strength of his heart, through every danger and difficulty. The perfect devotee can be harmed by none: no weapon can slay him, no water can drown him. He is one with the Spirit Immortal, for love is immortal life. Therefore, said Nârada, and I finish with him as I began with him,—"Its nature is supreme devotion to some one. Love is immortal."

Oh! for such a man to help us! for such a man to teach us! We cannot yet become it, we cannot be the love that makes us God; but might we not by our love help others who are worthier, might we not press on the progress of those who have advanced further? Remember that many a little stream joined together may form a mighty torrent. Let us bring our rills of love and adoration to the feet of the Supreme. Let us give our love, however feeble; let us give our aspiration, however halting; let us give our devotion, however weak; let us place them at His feet who is Love, who is pure Good. Might it not be that out of our many loves a great flame of love should arise that should help our land, that should purify our people? While the aspiration is here, the result is a possibility. Let it be ours to do something for that great work.

DHARMA

THREE LECTURES

Delivered at the Eighth Annual Convention of the Indian Section of the Theosophical Society held at Benares on October 25th, 26th, and 27th, 1898

DHARMA

DIFFERENCES

WHEN the nations of the earth were sent forth one after the other, a special word was given by God to each, the word which each was to say to the world, the peculiar word from the Eternal which each one was to speak. As we glance over the history of the nations, we can hear resounding from the collective mouth of the people this word, spoken out in action, the contribution of that nation to the ideal and perfect humanity. To Egypt in old days, the word was Religion; to Persia the word was Purity; to Chaldea the word was Science; to Greece the word was Beauty; to Rome the word was Law; and to India, the eldest-born of His children, to India He gave a word that summed up the whole in one, the word *DHARMA*. That is the word of India to the world.

But we cannot speak this word, so full of meaning, so vast in its out-reaching force, without making our obeisance at the feet of him who is the greatest embodiment of Dharma that the world has ever seen—Bhîshma, the son of Gangâ, the mightiest incarnation of Duty. Come with me for a while, travelling five thousand years back in time, and see this hero, lying on his bed of arrows on the field of Kurukshetra, there holding Death at bay, until the right hour should strike. We pass through heaps upon heaps of the slaughtered warriors, over mountains of dead elephants and horses, and we pass by many a funeral pyre, many a pile of broken weapons and chariots. We come to the hero lying on the bed of arrows, transfixed with hundreds of arrows and his head resting on a pillow of arrows. For he has rejected the pillows they brought him of soft down, and accepted only the arrowy pillow made by Arjuna. He, perfect in Dharma, had, while still a youth, for the sake of his father, for the sake of the duty that he owed to his father, for the sake of the love he bore to his father, made that great vow of renouncing family life, renouncing the crown, in order that the father's will might be done, and the father's heart be satisfied. And Shântanu gave him his blessing, that wondrous boon, that death should not come to him until it came at his own command, until he willed to die. When he fell, pierced by hundreds of arrows, the sun was in his southern path, and the season was not favourable for the death of one who was not to return any more. He used the power that his father had given him, and made death stand aside until the sun should open up the way to eternal peace and liberation. As he lay there for many a weary day, racked with the agonies of his wounds, tortured by the anguish of the mangled body that he wore, there came around him many Rishis and the remnants of the Aryan kings, and thither came also Shrî Krishṇa, to see the faithful one. Thither came the five princes, the sons of Pâṇḍu, the victors in the mighty war, and they stood round him weeping and worshipping him, and longing to be taught by him. To him, in the midst of that bitter anguish, came the words from One whose lips were the lips of God, and He released him from the burning fever, and He gave him bodily rest and clearness of mind and quietness of the inner man, and then He bade him teach to the world what Dharma is—he whose whole life had taught it, who had not swerved from the path of righteousness, who, whether as son, or prince, or statesman, or warrior, had always trodden the narrow path. He was asked for teaching by those who were around him, and Vâsudeva bade him speak of Dharma, because he was fit to teach.*

* *Mahâbhârata*, Shânti Parva, § LIV.

Then there drew closer round him the sons of Pâṇḍu, headed by their eldest brother Yudhishṭhira, who was the leader of the host that had brought Bhîshma to his death; and he was afraid of coming near and asking questions, thinking that as the arrows were really his, being shot for his cause, he was guilty of the blood of his elder, and he ought not to ask to be taught. Seeing his hesitation, Bhîshma, whose mind was ever balanced, who had trodden the difficult path of duty without being moved to the right hand or the left, spoke the memorable words: "As the duty of Brâhmaṇas consists in the practice of charity, study, and penance, so the duty of Kshattriyas is to cast away their bodies in battle. A Kshattriya should slay sires and grandsires and brothers and preceptors and relatives and kinsmen, that may engage with him in unjust battle. This is their declared duty. That Kshattriya, O Keshava, is said to be acquainted with his duty who slays in battle his very preceptors, if they happen to be sinful and covetous and disregardful of restraints and vows . . . . Ask me, O child, without any anxiety." Then, just as Vâsudeva, in speaking of Bhîshma, had described Bhîshma's right to speak as teacher, so Bhîshma himself in turn, in addressing the princes, described the qualities that were needed in those who would ask questions on the problem of Dharma:

"Let the son of Pâṇḍu, in whom are intelligence, self-restraint, Brahmacharya, forgiveness, righteousness, mental vigour and energy, put questions to me. Let the son of Pâṇḍu, who always by his good offices honours his relatives and guests and servants and others that are dependent on him, put questions to me. Let the son of Pâṇḍu, in whom are truth and charity and penances, heroism, peacefulness, cleverness and fearlessness, put questions to me." *

Such are some of the characteristics of the man who may seek to understand the mysteries of Dharma. Such are the qualities which you and I must try to develop, if we are to understand the teachings, if we are to be worthy to enquire.

Then began that wonderful discourse, without parallel among the discourses of the world. It treats of the duties of kings and of subjects, the duties of the four orders, of the four modes of life, duties of every kind of man, duties distinct from each other and suited to every stage of evolution. Every one of you ought to know that great discourse, ought to study it, not only for its literary beauty, but for its moral grandeur. If we could but follow on the path traced by Bhîshma, then would our evolution quicken, then would the day of India's redemption draw nearer to its dawn.

With regard to morality—a subject closely bound

* *Mahâbhârata*, Shânti Parva, § LV.

up with Dharma, and which cannot be understood without a knowledge of what is meant by Dharma —with regard to morality, some think that it is a simple thing. So it is in its broad outlines. The boundaries of right and wrong in the common actions of life are clear, simple, and definite. For a man of small development, for a man of narrow intelligence, for a man of restricted knowledge, morality seems simple enough. But for those of deep knowledge and high intelligence, for those who are evolving towards the higher grades of humanity, for those who desire to understand its mysteries, for them morality is very difficult: "morality is very subtle," as the prince Yudhishṭhira said when he was dealing with the problem of the marriage of Krishṇâ with the five sons of Pâṇḍu. And one greater than that prince had spoken of the difficulty; Shrî Krishṇâ, the Avatâra, in His discourse delivered on the field of Kurukshetra, spoke on this very question of the difficulty of action. He said:—

"What is action, what inaction? Even the wise are hereby perplexed. It is needful to discriminate action, to discriminate unlawful action, to discriminate inaction; mysterious is the path of action." *

Mysterious is the path of action; mysterious, because morality is not, as the simple-minded

* *Bhagavad Gîtâ*, iv. 16–17.

think, one and the same for all; because it varies with the Dharma of the individual. What is right for one is wrong for another. And what is wrong for one is right for another. Morality is an individual thing, and it depends upon the Dharma of the man who is acting, and not upon what is sometimes called "absolute right and wrong." There is nothing absolute in a conditioned universe. And right and wrong are relative, and must be judged in relation to the individual and his duties. Thus the greatest of all Teachers said with regard to Dharma—and this will guide us in our tangled path—"Better one's own Dharma, though destitute of merit, than the Dharma of another well-discharged. Better death in the discharge of one's own Dharma; the Dharma of another is full of danger." *

He repeated the same thought again at the end of that immortal discourse, and He said—but then changed in such a way as to throw fresh light on the subject—"Better is one's own Dharma, though destitute of merits, than the well-executed Dharma of another. He who doeth the Karma laid down by his own nature incurreth not sin." † There He expounds more fully this teaching, and He traces for us one by one the Dharma of the four great castes, and the very wording that He uses shows us the meaning of this word, which is sometimes

* *Bhagavad Gîtâ*, iii. 35. † *Bhagavad Gîtâ*, xviii. 47.

translated as Duty, sometimes as Law, sometimes as Righteousness, sometimes as Religion. It means these, and more than any of them, for the meaning is deeper and wider than any of these words expresses. Let us take the words of Shrî Krishṇa when speaking of the Dharma of the four castes: —"Of Brâhmaṇas, Kshattriyas, Vaishyas, and Shûdras, O Parantapa, the Karmas have been distributed *according to the guṇas born of their own natures.* Serenity, self-restraint, austerity, purity, forgiveness, and also uprightness, wisdom, knowledge, belief in God, are the Brâhmaṇa-Karma, born of his own nature. Prowess, splendour, firmness, dexterity, and also not flying from battle, generosity, the nature of a ruler, are the Kshattriya-Karma, born of his own nature. Ploughing, protection of kine, and trade are the Vaishya-Karma, born of his own nature. Action of the nature of service is the Shûdra-Karma, born of his own nature. Man reacheth perfection by each being intent on his own Karma."

Then he goes on to say: "Better one's own Dharma, though destitute of merits, than the well-executed Dharma of another. He who doeth the Karma laid down by his own nature incurreth not sin."

See how the two words Dharma and Karma are interchanged. They give us the key which we shall use to unlock our problem. Let me give you first a partial definition of Dharma. I cannot make the whole definition clear at once. I will give you the first half of it, dealing with the second half when we come to it. The first half is that "Dharma is the inner nature, which has reached in each man a certain stage of development and unfolding." It is this inner nature which moulds the outer life, which is expressed by thoughts, words, and actions, the inner nature which is born into the environment suited for its further growth. The first idea to grasp is that Dharma is not an outer thing, like the law, or righteousness, or religion, or justice. It is the law of the unfolding life, which moulds all outside it to the expression of itself.

Now, in trying to trace out this difficult and abstruse subject, I will treat it under three main divisions. First, DIFFERENCES, for people have different Dharmas. Even in the passage quoted four great classes are mentioned. Looking more closely, each individual man has his own Dharma. How shall we understand these? Unless we grasp something of the nature of differences, why they came to be, why they should exist, and what we mean when we speak of differences; unless we understand how each man shows by his thoughts, words, and actions, the stage he has reached: unless we grasp this, we cannot understand Dharma. Then, secondly, we shall have to deal with EVOLUTION. For we must trace these differences as they evolve. Lastly, we must deal with the problem of RIGHT and WRONG, for the whole of our study leads up to the answer to the question: "How should a man conduct his life?" It would not be worth while to ask you to follow me into difficult regions of thought, unless in the end we are to turn our knowledge to good account, and try to lead lives according to Dharma, thus giving to the world that which India was meant to teach.

In what does the perfection of a universe consist? When we begin to think over a universe and what we mean by it, we find we mean a vast number of separated objects working together more or less harmoniously. Variety is the key-note of the universe, as unity is the note of the Unmanifest, of the Unconditioned—the One without a second. Diversity is the note of the manifested and conditioned—the result of the will to become many.

When a universe is to come into existence, we learn, the First Cause, the Eternal, the Inconceivable, the Indiscernible, the Subtle, shines forth by His own Will. What that shining forth may mean within Himself none may dare to guess. What it means on the side from which we regard it, that to some extent may be grasped. Îshvara comes forth. But He, coming forth, appears enwrapped in the veil of Mâyâ—there are two sides of the Supreme in manifestation. Many words have been used to express that fundamental pair of opposites: Îshvara and Mâyâ, Sat and Asat, Reality and Unreality, Spirit and Matter, Life and Form. These are words which we, in our limited language, use to express that which is well-nigh beyond the grasp of thinking. All that we can say is: "Thus have the Sages taught us, and thus we in humility repeat."

Îshvara and Mâyâ. What is the universe to be? It is the image of Îshvara reflected in Mâyâ—the perfected image of Îshvara, as He has chosen to condition himself for this particular universe whose birth hour is come. His image—limited, conditioned. His self-conditioned image, the universe is in perfection to declare. But how shall that which is limited, that which is partial, image Îshvara? By the multiplicity of parts working together in one harmonious whole; infinite variety of differences, and the manifold combinations of each with each, shall speak forth the law of the divine thought, until the whole thought is expressed in the totality of that perfected universe. You should try to catch some glimpse of what this means. Let us together seek to understand.

Îshvara thinks of Beauty; at once His mighty energy, all-potent, generative, strikes upon Mâyâ, and develops it into myriad forms of objects that we call beautiful. It touches the matter that is ready to be moulded—for example, water; and the water takes on a million forms of beauty. We see one in the vast expanse of ocean, still and tranquil, where no wind is blowing, and where the sky is mirrored in its deep bosom. Then we catch another form of Beauty, when the wind lashes it into billows upon billows, and abyss beneath abyss, till the whole mass is terrible in its fury and grandeur. Then a new form of Beauty comes forth from it, and the raging and the foaming waters are hushed, and the ocean is changed into myriad ripples, glittering and glistening under the moon which shines upon them, her rays broken and bent into a thousand corruscations. And this gives us another hint of what Beauty means. And then we look at the ocean where no land limits the horizon and where the vast expanse is unbroken, and again we stand on the shore and see the waves breaking at our feet. With every change of mood of the sea, its waters speak out a new thought of Beauty. Another glimpse of the thought of Beauty thrown into water we see in the mountain lake, in the stillness and serenity of its quiet bosom; and in the stream that leaps from rock to rock; and in the torrent that dashes itself into millions of spray-drops, catching and refracting the sunlight into all the hues of the rainbow. So from water in every shape and form, from the tossing ocean to the frozen iceberg, from the foggy mists to the gorgeously coloured clouds, bursts forth the thought of Beauty impressed upon it by Îshvara, when the word came forth from Him. When we leave the water, we learn new thoughts of beauty in the tender creeper, in its mass of brilliant colours, in the stronger plant and the sturdier oak, and the dark obscurity of forest depths. New thoughts of beauty come to us from the face of every mountain peak, and from the vast rolling prairie, where the earth seems to break into new possibilities of life, from the sand of the desert, from the green of the meadow. If we are tired of the earth, the telescope brings to our view the beauty of myriads of suns, rushing and rolling through the depths of space. Then the microscope reveals to our wondering gaze the beauty of the infinitely small, as the telescope does of the infinitely great: and thus a new door is opened to us for the contemplation of Beauty. Around us we have thousands and millions of objects that are all beautiful. From the grace of the animal, from the strength of man, from the supple beauty of woman, from the dimples of the laughing children, from all these things we catch some glimpses of what the thought of Beauty is in the mind of Îshvara.

In this fashion we may sense something of the way in which His thought broke into myriad forms of splendour, when He spoke as Beauty to the world. The same in the case with Strength, Energy, Harmony, Music, and so on. You grasp, then, why there should be variety; because no limited thing may fully tell Him, because no limited form may fully express Him. But as each becomes perfect of its kind, all combined may partly reveal Him. Thus the perfection of the Universe is perfection in variety and in the harmony of inter-related parts.

Having reached that conception, we begin to see that the Universe can only gain perfection by each part performing its own function, and developing completely its own share of life. If the tree tries to imitate the mountain, or the water to imitate the earth, each would miss its own beauty and fail to show that of the other. The perfection of the body does not depend upon every cell doing the work of the other cells, but in each cell doing its own part perfectly. We have brain, lungs, heart, digestive organs, and so on. If the brain tried to do the work of the heart, and the lungs tried to digest food, then the body would indeed be in a melancholy condition. The health of the body is secured by each organ doing its own part. We thus realise that as the Universe develops, each part is going along the road which is marked out by the law of its own life. The image of Îshvara in nature will never be perfect, until each part is complete in itself and in its relations to the others.

How can these innumerable differences arise?

How can all these differences come into existence? How does the Universe, as it evolves as a whole, stand in relation to its parts evolving each on its separate line? We are told that Îshvara, expressing himself on the Prakriti side, shows forth three qualities—Sattva, Rajas, and Tamas. No English words are equivalent to or can satisfactorily translate these. I may, however, for the moment translate Tamas as inertia, the quality that does not move, that gives stability; Rajas is the quality of energy and motion; and Sattva is perhaps best expressed by harmony, the quality of pleasure-giving, as all pleasure springs from harmony and only harmony can give it. Then we learn that these three guṇas are further modified in seven kinds of ways—seven great lines, as it were, along which innumerable combinations evolve. Every religion speaks of this sevenfold division, every religion proclaims its existence. In Hinduism, they are the five great elements and the two beyond. These are the seven Purushas of whom Manu speaks.

These three guṇas combine and divide, arranging themselves into seven great groups, from which arise vast numbers of things by various combinations; remember that into each separate thing each of these qualities enters in different proportions, modified in one of the seven fundamental ways.

From this primary difference brought over from a universe of the past—for world is linked to world and universe to universe—we find that the downpouring life divided and subdivided itself as it fell into matter, till, reaching the circumference of the mighty circle, it rolled back upon itself. Evolution begins at the turning-point where the wave of life begins to return to Îshvara. The previous stage is the stage of involution, during which this life is becoming involved in matter; in evolution it is unfolding the powers that it contains. We may quote Manu where he says that Îshvara placed His seed in the mighty waters. The life which Îshvara gave was not a developed life, but a life capable of development. Everything exists in germ at first. As the parent gives his life to generate the child, and as that life-seed is built up through many combinations until it reaches birth, and then year after year, through childhood, youth, and manhood, until maturity is reached, and the image of the father is seen again in the son; so does the Eternal Father, when He places the seed in the womb of matter, give the life, but it is not yet evolved. Then it begins its up-climbing, bringing out one phase after another of the life that it is gradually becoming able to express.

As we study the Universe, we find that its varieties differ in their age. This is a thought which bears upon our problem. This world was not brought into its present condition by one creative word. Slowly and gradually and by prolonged meditation did Brahmâ make the world. One after another living forms came forth. One after another the seeds of life were sown. If you look at any universe at any point of time, you will find that the variety of that universe has Time for its chief factor. The age of the developing germ will mark the stage at which that germ has arrived. In a universe, at one and the same time, there are germs of various ages and stages of development. There are germs younger than minerals, making what are called elemental kingdoms. The developing germs called the mineral kingdom are older than these. Germs evolving as the vegetable world are older than those of the mineral, that is, they have a longer stretch of evolution behind them; the animals are germs with a yet longer past, and the germs we call humanity have the longest past of all.

Each great class has this diversity as to its beginning in time. So also the separated individual life in one man—not the essential life, but the individual and separated life—is different from that of another, and we differ in the age of our individual existences as we differ in the age of our bodies. The life is one—one life in all; but it is infolded at different stages of time, as regards the starting-point of the seed that there is growing. You should grasp that idea clearly. When a universe comes to its ending, there will be present in it entities at every stage of growth. I have already said that world is linked to world, and universe linked to universe. Some units at the beginning will be at an early stage of evolution; some will be ready to expand ere long into the consciousness of God. In the Universe, when its life-period is over, there will be all the differences of growth dependent upon differences in time. There is one life in all, but the stage of enfoldment of a particular life depends upon the time through which it has been separately evolving. There you grasp the very root of our problem—one life, undying, eternal, infinite as to its source and goal; but that life manifesting itself in different grades of evolution, and at different stages of unfoldment, different amounts of its inherent powers showing forth according to the age of the separated life. Those are the two thoughts to grasp, and then you can take the other portion of the definition of Dharma.

Dharma may now be defined as the "inner nature of a thing at any given stage of evolution, and the law of the next stage of its unfolding"—the nature at the point it has reached in unfolding, and then the law which brings about its next stage of unfolding. The nature itself marks out the point in evolution it has reached; then comes what it must do in order to evolve further along its road. Take those two thoughts together, and then you will understand why perfection must be reached by following one's own Dharma. My Dharma is the stage of evolution which my nature has reached in unfolding the seed of divine life which is myself, *plus* the law of life according to which the next stage is to be performed by me. It belongs to this separated self. I must know the stage of my growth, and I must know the law which will enable me to grow further; then I know my Dharma, and by following that Dharma, I am going towards perfection.

It is clear, then, realising what this means, why we should each of us study this present condition and this next stage. If we do not know the present stage, we must be ignorant of the next stage which we should aim at, and we may be going against our Dharma and thus delaying our evolution. Or, knowing both, we may work with our Dharma and quicken our evolution. Here comes a great pit-fall. We see that a thing is good, noble, and great, and we long to accomplish in ourselves that thing. Is it for us the next stage of evolution? Is it the thing which the law of our unfolding life demands, in order that that life may unfold harmoniously? Our immediate aim is not that which is best in itself, but that which is best for us in our present stage, and carries us one step onward. Take a child. There is no doubt that if you take a woman-child, she has before her a future nobler, higher, and more beautiful than the present when she is playing with her dolls; she will be a mother with a baby in her arms instead of a doll; for that is the ideal of perfect womanhood—the mother with the child. But while that is the ideal of a perfect woman, to grasp at that ideal before the time is ripe will do harm and not good. Everything must come in its proper time and place. If that mother is to be developed to the perfection of womanhood, and is to be the mother of a family, healthy, strong, able to bear the pressure of the great life-stream, then there must be the period when that child must play with her dolls, must learn lessons, must develop the body. But if, thinking that motherhood is higher and nobler than play, that motherhood should be grasped before its time, and a child be born from a child, the babe suffers, the mother suffers, the nation suffers; and this because the season has not been regarded, the law of unfolding life is violated. All sorts of suffering arise from grasping the fruit ere the fruit is ripe.

I take that example because it is a striking one. It will help you to see why our own Dharma is better for us than the well-executed Dharma of another that is not in the line of our unfolding life.

That lofty post may be for us in the future, but the time must come, the fruit must ripen. Pluck it ere it is ripe, and your teeth are set on edge. Let it remain on the tree, obeying the law of time and sequential evolution, and the soul will grow according to the power of an endless life.

That then gives us another key to the problem—function is in relation to power. Function grasped before power is developed is mischievous in the extreme to the organism. So we learn the lessons of patience and of waiting on the Good Law. You might judge the progress of a man by his willingness to work with nature and to submit to the law. That is why Dharma is spoken of as law, and sometimes as duty; for both these ideas grow out of the root-thought that it is the inner nature at a given stage of evolution and the law of the next stage of its development. This explains why morality is relative, why duty must differ for every soul, according to the stage of its evolution. When we come to apply this to questions of right and wrong, we shall find that we can solve some of the subtlest problems of morality by dealing with them on this principle. In a conditioned universe, absolute right and wrong are not to be found, but only relative rights and wrongs. The absolute is in Îshvara alone, where it will for ever be found.

Differences are thus necessary for our conditioned consciousness. We think by differences, we feel by differences, and we know by differences. It is only by differences that we know that we are living and thinking men. Unity makes on consciousness no impression. Differences and diversities—those are the things which make the growth of consciousness possible. The unconditioned consciousness is beyond our thinking. We can only think within the limits of the separated and the conditioned.

We can now see how differences in nature come to be, how the time factor comes in, and how, though all have the same nature and will reach the same goal, yet there are differences in the stages of manifestation, and therefore in the laws appropriate for every stage. That is what we need to grasp to-night, before we deal with the complex problem, how this inner nature develops. Truly difficult is the subject, yet the mysteries of the path of action may be cleared for us as we grasp the underlying law, as we recognise the principle of the unfolding life.

May He, who gave Dharma to India as her key-note, illuminate with His unfolding and immortal life, with His light, effulgent and unchangeable, these dark minds of ours that dimly try to grasp His law; for only as His blessing falls upon the suppliant seeker, will His law be understood by the mind, will His law be engraven in the heart.

EVOLUTION

WE shall deal this evening with the second section of the subject commenced yesterday. You may remember I divided the subject under three heads, for the sake of convenience—Differences, Evolution, and the problem of Right and Wrong. Yesterday we studied the question of Differences—how it came to pass that different men had different Dharmas. I will venture to remind you of the definition of Dharma we adopted; that it means the inner nature, marked by the stage of evolution, *plus* the law of growth for the next stage of evolution. I will ask you to keep that definition in your minds, for without it you will not be able to apply Dharma to what we are to study under the third division of the subject.

Under the head "Evolution" we are to study the way in which the germ of life evolves to the perfect image of God, remembering that we found that that image of God could only be represented by the totality of the numerous objects making up the universe in their details, and that the perfection of the individual depended on the completeness with which he fulfilled his own part in the stupendous whole.

Before we can understand evolution, we must find its spring and motive—a life which involves itself in matter, before it evolves complicated organisms of every kind. We start with the principle that all is from and in God. Nothing in the universe is to be excluded from Him. No life save His life, no force save His force, no energy save His energy, no forms save His forms—all are the results of His thought. That is our fundamental position. That is the ground on which we must stand, daring to accept everything that it implies, daring to recognise everything that it connotes. "The seed of all beings," says Shrî Krishṇa, speaking as the supreme Îshvara, "that am I, O Arjuna! nor is there aught, moving or unmoving, that may exist bereft of Me."* Do not let us fear to take that central position. Do not, because of the imperfection of the evolving lives, let us shrink from any conclusion to which this truth may lead us.

In another shloka He said: "I am the gambling of the cheat, and the splendour of splendid things, I."† What is the meaning of these words

* *Bhagavad Gîtâ*, x. 39.

† *Bhagavad Gîtâ*, x. 36.

that sound so strange? What is the explanation of this phrase which appears almost as profanity? Not only in this discourse do we find this position enunciated, but we find that Manu teaches exactly the same truth :—" From Himself He produces the universe." The life coming forth from the Supreme puts on veil after veil of Mâyâ, in which that life is to evolve all the perfections that lie latent within it.

Now the first question is: Does not this life, which comes from Îshvara, already contain within itself everything already developed, every manifested power, every possibility realised as actuality? The answer to that question, spoken over and over again, in symbols, allegories, and distinct words, is "No." It contains everything in potency, but nothing at first in manifestation. It contains everything in germ, but nothing at first as developed organism. The seed is that which is placed in the mighty waters of matter, the germ alone is given forth by the Life of the world. Those germs, which come from the life of Îshvara, evolve—step by step, stage after stage, on one rung of a ladder after another—all the powers that reside in the generating Father, the name that Îshvara gives to Himself in the *Gîtâ*. He declares once more:—"My womb is the Mahat-Brahma ; in that I place the germ ; thence cometh the production of all beings, O Bhârata.

In whatsoever wombs mortals are produced, O Kaunteya, the Mahat-Brahma is their womb, I their generating father."* From that seed, from that germ containing everything in possibility but nothing as yet in manifestation—from that seed is to evolve a life, stage by stage, rising higher and higher, until at last a centre of consciousness is formed capable of expanding to the consciousness of Îshvara, while remaining as a centre still, with the power to come forth as a new Logos, or Îshvara, for the production of a new universe.

Let us take this vast sweep of thought in detail. Life involved in matter—that is our beginning. These germs of life, these myriad seeds, or, to use the Upanished phrase, these numberless sparks, all come forth from the one Flame which is the supreme Brahman. Qualities are now to be brought out of these seeds. Those qualities are powers, but powers manifested through matter. One by one those powers will be brought out—powers which are the life of Îshvara as veiled in Mâyâ. Slow is the growth in the early stages, hidden as the seed underground is hidden, when first it strikes its root downward, and sends its tender offshoot upward in order that later on the growing tree may appear. In silence germinates this divine seed, and the early beginnings are

* *Bhagavad Gîtâ*, xiv. 3-4.

hidden in darkness, like the roots under the ground.

This power in the life, or rather these innumerable powers which Îshvara manifests in order that the universe may be, these myriad powers are at first unapparent in the germ—no sign of the mighty possibilities, no trace of what it is hereafter to become. A word is spoken as to this manifestation in matter, which throws much light on the subject, if we can grasp its inner and subtler meaning. Shrî Krishṇa, speaking of His lower Prakriti, or inferior manifestation, says: "Earth, water, fire, air, ether, Manas and Buddhi also and Ahankâra—these are the eightfold division of My Prakriti—This the inferior." Then he says what is His higher Prakriti: "Know My other Prakriti, the higher, the life-element, O mighty-armed, by which the universe is upheld."* Then a little later, separated by many shlokas, so that sometimes the connecting link is missed, other words are spoken. "This divine Mâyâ of Mine, Guṇa-made, is hard to pierce; they who come to Me they cross over this Mâyâ."† This Yoga-Mâyâ is, truly, hard to pierce; many do not discover Him involved in Mâyâ, so hard to pierce it is, so difficult to discover. "Those without Buddhi think of Me, the unmanifest, as having manifestation; knowing not My supreme nature,

* *Bhagavad Gîtâ*, vii. 4, 5. † *Bhagavad Gîtâ*, vii. 14.

imperishable, most excellent. Nor am I of all discovered, enveloped in My Yoga-Mâyâ."* Then He further declares that by His unmanifested life it is that the universe is pervaded. The life-element, or higher Prakriti, is unmanifested, the lower Prakriti is manifested. Then He says: "From the unmanifested all the manifested stream forth at the coming of day; at the coming of night they dissolve, even in That called the unmanifested."† This occurs over and over again. Then further on He declares: "Therefore verily there existeth, higher than that unmanifested, another unmanifested, eternal, which, in the destroying of all beings, is not destroyed.‡ There is a subtle distinction between Îshvara and the image of Himself which He sends forth. The image is the reflected unmanifest, but Himself is the higher unmanifest, the eternal that never is destroyed.

Realising that, we come to the drawing out of powers. Here we begin really our evolution. The out-pouring life was involved in matter, in order to bring the seed into the matter-surrounded conditions which should make evolution possible. When we come to the first germinating of the seed, our difficulty comes in. For we must throw ourselves, in thought, to the time when there was no

* *Bhagavad Gîtâ*, vii. 24, 25. † *Bhagavad Gîtâ*, viii. 18.
‡ *Bhagavad Gîtâ*, viii. 20.

reason in this embryonic self, no imaginative faculty, no memory, no judgment, none of the conditioned faculties of the mind that we know; when all the life that was manifested was that which we find in the mineral kingdom, with the lowest conditions of consciousness. The minerals manifest consciousness by their attractions and repulsions, by their holding together of particles, by their affinities for each other, by their repellings of each other, but they show none of that consciousness that can be called the recognition of the "I" and the "not-I."

In every one of these lowest forms in the mineral kingdom, Îshvara's life is beginning to unfold. Not only is the germ of life there evolving, but He, in all His might and power, is there in every atom of His universe. His the moving life which makes evolution inevitable. His the force expanding gently the walls of matter, with immense patience and watching love, in order that they may not break under the strain. God, Himself the Father of the life, holds that life within Himself as Mother, unfolding the seed unto the likeness of Himself, never impatient, never hurrying, willing to give as much time from the countless ages as the little germ may require. Time is nothing to Îshvara, for He is eternal, and to him all IS. It is the perfection of manifestation that He seeks, and there is no hurrying in His work. And we shall see, later on, how this infinite patience works out. The man, who is to be the image of his Father, shows within him the reflection of the Self with which he is one, and whence he came.

The life is to be awakened, but how? By blows, by vibrations, the inner essence is called into activity. Life is stirred to activity by vibrations that touch it from outside. These myriad seeds of life, not yet conscious of themselves, matter-enveloped, are thrown against each other in the myriad processes of nature; but "nature" is only the garment of God, is only the lowest manifestation in which He shows Himself on the material plane. These forms strike against each other, shaking thus the outer shells of matter in which the life is involved, and the life within gives a quiver as the blow is delivered.

Now the nature of the blow is of no importance. All that is important is that the blow shall be strong. Any experience is useful. Anything which strikes that shell so forcibly that the life within quivers in response is all that is wanted at first. The life within must be made to quiver. That will awaken some dawning power in the life. At first it is only a quiver within itself, and nothing more than a quiver, with no result on its outer shell. But as blow after blow is repeated, and vibration after vibration sends in its earthquake shocks, the life within sends out, through its own enveloping shell, a thrill of answer. The blow has provoked an answer. Another stage is thus touched—the answer comes forth from the hidden life and goes out beyond the shell. This goes on through the mineral kingdom and the vegetable kingdom. In the vegetable kingdom the answers to the vibrations caused by contact begin to show a new power of the life—sensation. The life begins to show out in itself what we call "feeling"; that is, different answers are given to pleasure and to pain. Pleasure is fundamentally harmonious. All that gives pleasure is harmonious. All that gives pain is discordant. Think of music. Rhythmical notes, struck together as a chord, give to the ear a sensation of pleasure. But if you strike your finger on the strings without paying attention to the notes, you make a discord, which gives pain to the ear. That which is true of music is true everywhere. Health is harmony, disease is discord. Strength is harmony, weakness is discord. Beauty is harmony, ugliness is discord. All through nature pleasure means the answer of a sentient being to vibrations that are harmonious and rhythmical, and pain means its answer to those that are discordant and unrhythmical. The rhythmical vibrations make an outward channel through which the life can expand, and this pouring forth is "pleasure"; the unrhythmical close up the channels and frustrate the forthpouring, and this frustration is "pain."* The forthpouring of life towards objects is what we name "desire"; hence pleasure becomes the gratification of desire. This difference begins to make itself felt in the vegetable kingdom. A blow comes that is harmonious. The life answers to that in harmonious vibrations and expands, feeling in that expansion "pleasure." A blow comes that is a jangle. Life answers to that discordantly, is checked, and feels in that check "pain." The blows are given over and over again, and not until the repetition has occurred a myriad times does a recognition of the distinction between the two begin to arise in that imprisoned life. Only by making distinctions is our consciousness, as at present constituted, able to distinguish objects from each other. Take a very common illustration. Let a piece of money lie in the palm of the hand and close your fingers round it; you feel it; but as the pressure is continued, without any variation, the sensation of feeling in the hand disappears and you do not know that your hand is not empty. Move a finger and you feel the money; keep the hand still, and the sensation vanishes. Thus consciousness can only know things by differences. And when difference is eliminated, consciousness ceases to respond.

* The student should work out in detail this fundamental principle; he will thereby much clarify his thoughts.

We come to the next thing which is manifested as the life evolves through the animal kingdom. Pleasure and pain are now acutely felt, and a germ of recognition, connecting objects and sensations, begins; we call it "perception." What does this mean? It means that the life develops the power of forming a link between the object that impresses it and the sensation by which it responds to the object. When that dawning life, contacting an external object, knows it as an object that gives pleasure or pain, then we say that the object is perceived, and the faculty of perception, or the making of links between the outer and the inner worlds, is evolved; when that is established, mental power begins to germinate and to grow within that organism; we find it in the higher animals.

Let us take it in the savage man, where we shall be able to pass more rapidly over these early stages. We find the consciousness of "I" and "not-I" slowly establishing itself in him—the two going together. "Not-I" touches him, and "I" feels it; "not-I" gives him pleasure, and "I" knows it; "not-I" gives him pain, and "I" suffers it. A distinction is now being made between the feeling, thought of as "I," and all that causes it, thought of as "Not-I." Here commences intelligence, and the root of self-consciousness is beginning to develop. That is, *a centre* is being formed, to which everything goes in and from which everything comes out.

I spoke of repetition of vibrations, and now repetition produces results more rapidly. As repetition causes the perception of pleasure-giving objects, the next stage is developed, the expectation of pleasure before the contact takes place. The object is recognised as one that has given pleasure on previous occasions; a repetition of the pleasure is expected, and that expectation is the dawn of memory and the beginning of imagination, the interweaving of intellect with desire. Because the object has given pleasure before it is expected to give pleasure again. Thus expectation brings into manifestation another germinating quality of the mind. When we have the recognition of the object and the expectation of pleasure from its return, the next stage is the making and vivifying of a mental image of that object—the memory of it—thus causing an outflow of desire, desire to have that object, a longing for that object, and finally a going forth in search of that object that gives pleasurable sensation. Thus the man becomes full of active desires. He desires pleasure and is moved to seek it by the mind. For a long time he had remained in the animal stage, when he would never seek for a thing unless the actual sensation in his inner body made him want something that the outer world alone could satisfy. Just for one moment return to the animal; think what stirs the animal to action. A craving to get rid of an unpleasant sensation. He feels hunger, he desires food, and he goes in search of it; he feels thirst, he desires to quench it, and he goes in search of water. Thus he always goes in search of the object that will gratify the desire. Give him the gratification of desire and he is quiet. There is no self-initiated motion in the animal. The push must come from outside. True, the hunger is in the inner body, but that is outside the centre of consciousness. The evolution of consciousness may be traced by the proportion which the outside stimulus to action bears to the self-initiated stimulus. The lower consciousness is stimulated to activity by impulses coming from outside itself. The higher consciousness is stimulated to activity by motion initiated within.

Now, as we deal with our savage man, we find that the gratification of desire is the law of his progress. How strange that sounds to many of you. Says Manu: seeking to get rid of desires by gratifying them is like trying to quench the fire by pouring butter over it. Desire must be curbed and restrained. Desire is to be extinguished utterly. This is most certainly true, but only when a man has reached a certain stage of evolution. In the early stages, the gratification of desires is the law of evolution. If he does not gratify his desires, no growth for him is possible. You must realise that at that stage there is nothing which can be called morality. There is no distinction between right and wrong. Every desire should be gratified; when this commencing centre of self-consciousness is seeking to gratify desires, then alone it grows. In this lowest stage the Dharma of the savage man, or of the higher animal, is imposed on him. He does not choose; his inner nature, marked by the development of desire, demands gratification. The law of his growth is the satisfaction of these desires. So that the Dharma of the savage is the gratification of every desire. And you find in him no consciousness of right or wrong, not the faintest dawning notion that the gratification of desires is forbidden by some higher law.

Without that gratification of desires there is no further growth. All that growth must precede the dawning of reason and judgment and the development of the higher powers of memory and imagination. All these things must be evolved by the gratification of desire. Experience is the law of life, it is the law of growth. Unless he gathers experiences of every kind, he cannot know that he lives in a world of Law. Two ways does the law find for impressing itself on man: pleasure when the Law is followed, pain when the Law is opposed. If men did not at that early stage have every sort of experience, how could they learn of the existence of the Law? How can discrimination grow between right and wrong unless there is the experience of both good and evil? A universe can never come into existence except by the pairs of opposites, and these at one stage appear in the consciousness as good and evil. You cannot know light without darkness, motion without rest, pleasure without pain; so you cannot know the good that is harmony with the Law without knowing the evil that is discord with the Law. Good and evil are a pair of opposites in the later evolution of man, and man cannot become conscious of the difference between them unless he has experience of both.

Now we come to a change. Man has developed a certain power of discrimination. Left to himself utterly, he would come to know in time that some things help him on, that some things strengthen him, that some things increase his life; also that other things weaken him and diminish his life. Experience would teach him all that. Left only to the teaching of experience, he would come to know right from wrong, would identify the pleasure-giving that increased life with the right, and the pain-giving that diminished life with the wrong, and would thus reach the conclusion that all happiness and growth lay in obeying the Law. But it would take a very long time for this dawning intelligence to compare together experiences of pleasure and pain, and the confusing experiences in which that which at first gave pleasure became painful by excess, and then to deduce from them the principle of law. It would be a very long time before he could put innumerable experiences together, and deduce from them the idea that this thing is right, and that thing is wrong. But he is not left unaided to make that deduction. There come to him, from past worlds, Intelligences more highly evolved than his own, Teachers who come to help on his evolution, to train his growth, to tell him of the existence of a law determining that which will bring about his more rapid evolution, increasing his happiness, intelligence, and strength. In fact, Revelation from the mouth of a Teacher quickens evolution, and instead of man being left to the slow teaching of experience, the expression of the law from the mouth of a superior is made to assist his growth.

The Teacher comes and says to this dawning intelligence: "If you kill that man, you are doing an action that I forbid on divine authority. That action is *wrong*. It will bring misery." The Teacher says: "It is *right* to help the starving; that starving man is your brother; feed him, do not let him starve; share with him what you have. That action is *right*, and if you obey that law it will be well with you." Rewards of actions are held out to attract the dawning intelligence towards good, and punishments and threats to warn him from wrong. Earthly prosperity is joined with obedience of law, earthly misery with disobedience to law. This announcement of the law that misery follows on that which the law forbids, and happiness on that which the law commands, stimulates the dawning intelligence. He disregards the law, the penalty follows, and he suffers; and he says: "The Teacher told me so." Memory of a command proved by experience makes an impression on the consciousness far more quickly and more strongly than does experience alone without the revealed law. By this declaration of what the learned call the fundamental principles of morality, namely, that certain classes of actions retard evolution and other classes of action quicken evolution —by this declaration intelligence is immensely stimulated.

If man will not obey the law declared, then he is left to the hard teaching of experience. If he says: "I will have that thing, though the law forbid it," then he is left to the stern teaching of pain, and the whip of suffering teaches the lesson that he would not learn from the lips of love.

How often that happens now. How often a young man, argumentative and self-conceited, will not listen to law, will not listen to the experienced, pays no regard to the training of the past. Desire conquers intelligence. His father is heart-broken. "My son is plunged into vice," says he; "my son is going into evil. I instructed him in right conduct, and see, he has become a liar; my heart is broken for my son." But Îshvara, the Father more loving than any earthly father, has patience. For He is in the son as much as in the father. He is in him teaching him a lesson, in the only way by which that soul is willing to learn. He would not learn by authority or by example. At all hazards that desire for the evil thing which is stopping his evolution must be rooted out of his nature. If he will not learn by gentleness, let him then learn by pain. Let him learn by experience; let him plunge into vice, and reap the bitter pang that comes from trampling on the law. There is time; he will learn the lesson surely though painfully. God is in him, and still He lets him go that way; nay, He even opens the way that he may go along it; when he demands it, the answer of God is: "My child, if you will not listen, take your own way and learn your lesson in the fire of your agony and in the bitterness of your degradation. I am with you still, watching over you and your actions, the Fulfiller of the law and the Father of your life. You shall learn in the mire of degradation that cessation of desire which you would not learn from wisdom and from love." That is why He says in the *Gîtâ*: "I am the gambling of the cheat." For He is always patiently working for the glorious end, by rough ways if we will not walk in smooth. We, unable to understand that infinite compassion, misread Him, but He works on with the patience of eternity, in order that desire may be utterly uprooted, and His son may be perfect as his Father in heaven is perfect.

Let us go on the next stage. There are certain great laws of growth that are general. We have learned to look upon certain things as right and upon others as wrong. Every nation has its own standard of morality. Only a few know how that standard was formed, and where that standard fails. For ordinary affairs the standard is good enough. The experience of the race has found out, under the guidance of law, that some actions hold back evolution while others press it forward. The great law of the orderly evolution that follows the earlier stages is the law of the four successive steps in later human growth. This comes after a man has reached a certain point, after the preliminary training is over. It is found in every nation at a certain stage of evolution, but was proclaimed in ancient India as the definite law of evolving life, as the sequential order of the growth of the soul, as the underlying principle by which Dharma may be understood and followed.

Dharma, remember, includes two things—the inner nature at the point it has reached, and the law of its growth for the next stage. For every man Dharma is to be declared. The first Dharma is that of *service*. No matter in what land the souls may be born, when they have passed through the earlier stages, then their inner nature demands the discipline of service, and that they should learn by service the qualities that are needed for growth into the next stage. At this stage the power of independent action is very limited. At this comparatively early stage there is more tendency to yield to impulse from without than to show a developed judgment choosing a particular course from within. In this class are seen all those who belong to the serving type. Remember those wise words of Bhîshma, that if the characteristics of a Brâhmaṇa are found in a Shûdra and are not found in a Brâhmaṇa, then that Brâhmaṇa is not a Brâhmaṇa and that Shûdra is not a Shûdra. In other words, the characteristics of the inner nature mark out the stage of that soul's growth, and stamp it as belonging to one great natural division or another. Where the power of initiation is small, where the judgment is untrained, where the reason is poor and little developed, where the Self is unconscious of his high destiny, where he is chiefly moved by desire, where he is still to grow by the gratification of most but not all desires, that man is one whose Dharma is service, and only by performing that Dharma can he follow the law of growth by which he will reach perfection. And such a man is a Shûdra, by whatever name he may be called in different countries. In ancient India, the souls bearing the characteristics of this type were born into the classes that suited them, for Devas guided their births. In this age, however, confusion has supervened.

What is the law of growth in that stage? Obedience, devotion, fidelity. That is the law of growth for that stage. Obedience, because the judgment is not developed. He whose Dharma is service has to blindly obey the one to whom he renders service. His not to challenge the order of his superior, nor his to see that the commanded action is a wise one. He has received an order to do a thing, and his Dharma is obedience, by which alone he will be able to learn. People hesitate at that teaching, but it is true. I will take an example that will strike you most forcibly—that of an army, of a private soldier under the command of his captain. If every private soldier were to use his own judgment as to the orders that came from the general, and if he were to say: "This is not well, for in my judgment that is the place where I shall be more serviceable," what would become of the army? The private soldier is shot if he disobeys, for his duty is obedience. When your judgment is feeble, when you are chiefly moved by impulses from without, when you cannot be happy without noise and clatter and jangle around you, then your Dharma is service, wherever you may be born, and you are happy if your karma leads you to a position where discipline will train you.

So the man learns to prepare for the next stage. And the duty of all those who are in positions of authority is to remember that the Dharma of a Shûdra is fulfilled when he is obedient and faithful to his master, and they should not expect one in that grade of evolution to show forth the higher virtues. To demand from him cheerfulness in suffering, purity of thought, and the power to suffer hardships ungrudgingly, is to demand too much; for when we ourselves often do not show these qualities, how can we expect them from those whom we call the lower classes? The duty of the higher is to show forth the higher virtues, but he has no right to demand them from his inferiors. If the servant shows fidelity and obedience, his Dharma is perfectly performed, and other faults should not be punished, but should be gently pointed out by the master, for by so doing he is training that younger soul; for a child soul should be gently led along the path, and its growth should not be stunted by harsh treatment as we generally stunt it.

Then the soul, having learned this lesson in

many births, by learning the lesson has obeyed the law of growth, and by following his Dharma has approached the next stage, in which he is to learn the first use of power by acquiring wealth. Then the Dharma of that soul is to evolve all the qualities which are now ready for evolution, and are brought out by leading the life which the inner nature demands, *i.e.*, by taking up some occupation which the next stage requires, the stage where it is a merit to acquire wealth. For the Dharma of a Vaishya all over the world is to evolve certain definite faculties. The faculty of justice, just dealing between man and man, the not swerving aside at the mere prompting of sentiment, the working out of the qualities of shrewdness, keenness, and holding a just balance between contending duties, fair payment in fair exchange, acuteness of insight, frugality, absence of waste and extravagance, the exaction from every servant of the service that should be given, the payment of just wages but only of just wages—these are the characteristics which fit him for higher growth. It is a merit in the Vaishya to be frugal, to refuse to pay more than he should, to insist on a just and fair exchange. All these things bring out qualities that are wanted and will conduce to future perfection. In their early stages they are sometimes unlovely, but from the higher standpoint they are the Dharma of that man, and if it be not fulfilled, there will be weakness in the character, which will come out later and injure his evolution. Liberality is indeed the law of his further growth, but not the liberality of carelessness or of over-payment. He is to gather wealth by the exercise of frugality and strictness, and then to spend that wealth on noble objects and on learned men, to bestow it upon worthy and well-considered schemes for the public good. To gather with energy and shrewdness, and to spend with careful discrimination and liberality, that is the Dharma of a Vaishya, the outcome of his nature and the law of his further growth.

This leads us to the next stage, that of the rulers and warriors, of battles and struggles, where the inner nature is combative, aggressive, quarrelsome, standing on its own ground and ready to protect everyone in the enjoyment of what is right. Courage, fearlessness, splendid generosity, throwing away of life in the defence of the weak and in the discharging of one's duties—that is the Dharma of the Kshattriya. His duty is to protect what is given him in charge against all aggression from without. It may cost him life, but never mind that. He must do his duty. To protect, to guard, that is his work. His strength is to be a barrier between the weak and the oppressive, between the helpless and those who would trample them under foot. Right for him the following of war and the struggle in the jungle with the wild beast.

Because you do not understand what evolution is and what the law of growth, you stand aghast at the horrors of war. But the great Rishis, who made this order, knew that a weak soul can never attain perfection. You cannot get strength without courage, and firmness and courage cannot be got without the facing of danger, and the readiness to throw away life when duty demands the sacrifice.

Our sentimental, weak-kneed, pseudo-moralist shrinks from that teaching. But he forgets that in every nation there are souls that need that training, and whose further evolution depends upon their success in attaining it. I appeal again to Bhîshma, the incarnation of Dharma, and I remember what he said, that it is the duty of the Kshattriya to slay thousands of his enemies, if his duty in protection lies in that direction. War is terrible, fighting is shocking, our hearts revolt from it, and we shrink before the anguish of mutilated and mangled bodies. To a great extent this is because we are utterly deluded by form. The one use of the body is to enable the life within it to evolve. But the moment it has learned all that that body can give it, let the body break away, and let the soul go free to take a new body that will enable it to manifest higher powers. We cannot pierce the Mâyâ of the Lord. These bodies of ours may perish, time after time, but every death is a resurrection to higher life. This body itself is nothing more than a garment which the soul puts on, and no wise man would like the body to be eternal. We clothe our child in a small coat and change it when the child grows. But will you make the coat of iron, and cramp the growth of the child? So this body is our coat. Shall it be then of iron that it should never perish? Does not the soul require a new body for its higher growth? Let then the body go. This is the hard lesson the Kshattriya learns, and so he throws away his bodily life, and, in this throwing away, his soul gains the power of self-sacrifice, he learns endurance, fortitude, courage, resource, devotion to an ideal, loyalty to a cause, and he pays his body gladly as the price for these, the immortal soul rising triumphant and preparing for a nobler life.

Then there comes the last stage, the stage of teaching. The Dharma of that stage is to teach. The soul must have assimilated all lower experience before he can teach. If he had not been through all those previous stages, and obtained wisdom through obedience and exertion and combat, how could he be a teacher? He has reached the stage of evolution where the natural expansion of his inner nature is to teach his more ignorant brethren. These qualities are not artificial. They are inborn qualities of nature, and they show themselves wherever they exist. A Brâhmaṇa is not a Brâhmaṇa if he is not a teacher by his Dharma. He has gained knowledge and a favourable birth in order to make him a teacher.

The law of his growth is knowledge, piety, forgiveness, being the friend of every creature. How the Dharma is changed! But he could not be the friend of every creature if he had not learned to throw his life away when duty called, and the very battle trained the Kshattriya to become at a later stage the friend of every creature. What is the law of a Brâhmaṇa's growth? He must never take offence. He must never lose self-control. He must never be hasty. He must always be gentle: otherwise he falls from his Dharma. He must be all purity. He must never lead an evil life. He must detach himself from worldly things, if they have a hold upon him. Do I hold up an impossible standard? I but speak the law as the great ones have spoken it, and I but feebly re-echo their words. The law has laid down the Standard, and who shall dare to lower it? When Shrî Krishṇa Himself proclaimed that as the Dharma of the Brâhmaṇa, that must be the law of his growth, and the end of his growth is liberation. For him is liberation, but only if he shows out the qualities that he ought to have reached, and follows the lofty ideal that is his Dharma. These are the only justifications for the name of Brâhmaṇa.

This ideal is so beautiful that all earnest and thoughtful men desire to reach it. But wisdom steps in and says: "Yes, it shall be yours, but you must earn it. You must grow, you must labour; truly it is yours, but it is not yours until you have paid the price." Important is it for our own growth, and the growth of the nations, that this distinction in Dharmas should be understood as depending upon the stage of evolution, and that we should be able to discriminate our own Dharma by the characteristics which we find in our nature. If we set before an unprepared soul an ideal so lofty that it does not move him, we check his evolution. If you give to a peasant the ideal of a Brâhmaṇa, you are placing before him an impossible ideal, and the result is that he does nothing. When you tell a man a thing too high for him, that man knows that you have been talking nonsense, for you have commanded him to perform that which he has no power to perform; your folly has placed before him motives which do not move him. But wise were the teachers of old. They gave the children sugar plums, and later the higher lessons. But we are so clever, that we appeal to the lowest sinner by motives which can stir only the highest saint, and thus, instead of furthering, we check his evolution. Place your own ideal as high as you can set it; but do not impose your ideal upon your brother, the law of whose growth may be entirely different from yours. Learn the tolerance which helps each man to do in his place what it is good for him to do, and what his nature impels him to do. Leaving him in his place, help him. Learn that tolerance which is repelled by none, however sinful, which sees in every man a divinity working, and stands beside him to help him. Instead of standing off on some high peak of spirituality and preaching a doctrine of self-sacrifice, which is utterly beyond his comprehension, in teaching his young soul, use his higher selfishness to destroy the lower. Do not tell the peasant that when he is not industrious he is falling from the ideal; but tell that man: "There is your wife; you love that woman; she is starving. Set to work and feed her." By that motive, which is certainly selfish, you do more to raise that man than if you preach to him about Brahman, the unconditioned and unmanifest. Learn what Dharma means, and you will be of service to the world.

I do not wish to lower by one tiniest fraction your own ideal; you cannot aim too high. The fact that you can conceive it makes it yours, but does not make it that of your less developed younger brother. Aim at the loftiest you are able to think and to love. But, in aiming, consider the means as well as the end, your powers as well as your aspirations. Make your aspirations high. They are the germs of powers in your next life.

Through ever keeping the ideal high you will grow towards it, and what you long for to-day you shall be in the days to come. But have the tolerance of knowledge, and the patience which is divine. Each thing in its own place is in its right place. As the higher nature develops you can appeal to the qualities of self-sacrifice, purity and utter-self-devotion, to the will firmly fixed on God. That is the ideal for the highest to accomplish. Let us climb towards it gradually, lest we fail to reach it at all.

RIGHT AND WRONG

DURING the last two days of our study, we have been giving our attention and fixing our thought on what I may call the theoretical side, to a very great extent, of this complicated and difficult problem. We have tried to understand how the differences of nature arise. We have tried to grasp the sublime idea, that this world is intended to grow from the mere germ of life given out by God into the image of Him who gave it forth. The perfection of that image, we have seen, can only be gained by the multiplicity of finite objects, and perfection lies in that multiplicity; but in that same multiplicity we see is implied necessarily the limitation of each object. We then found that by the law of growth we must have existing in the universe, at one and the same time, every variety of inner evolving nature. As these natures are all at different stages of evolution, we cannot make on all of them the same demands, nor expect from all of them the discharge of the same functions.

Morality must be studied in relation to the people who are to practise it. In judging the standard of right and wrong for a particular individual, we must consider at what stage of growth that individual has arrived. Absolute right exists in Îshvarà alone; our right and wrong are relative, and depend for each of us very much on the stage of evolution that we have reached.

I am going to try this evening to apply this theory to the conduct of life. We must see whether we have gained, by the line of study that we have pursued, a rational and scientific idea of morality, so that we may no longer have the same confusion that is seen to-day. For we see that ideals are held up on one side as those which ought to be reproduced in life, and on the other hand we find that there is an absolute failure even to aim at these ideals; we behold a most unfortunate divergence between faith and practice. Morality is not without its laws; like everything else in the universe that is the expression of divine thought, morality has also its conditions and limitations. In this way it may be possible to bring a cosmos out of the present moral chaos, and to learn practical lessons in morality, which will enable India to grow, to develop, to become again an example to the world, reproducing her ancient grandeur, showing forth once more her ancient spirituality.

There are three recognised schools of morality existing among western people. We must remember that western thought is very largely influencing India, and especially is it influencing the rising generation, on which the hope of India rests. It is, therefore, necessary that we should understand something of these schools of morality, differing in their theories and teachings, that exist in the west, if it be only in order to learn to avoid their limitations, and to take from them whatever of good they may have to offer.

There is one school that says that revelation from God is the basis of morality. The objection raised by opponents to that statement is that in this world there are many religions, and every religion has its own revelation. Looking at this variety of religious scriptures, it is argued, it is difficult to say that one revelation is to be regarded as based on supreme authority. That each religion will regard its own revelation as supreme is natural, but in this conflict of tongues how shall a decision be made by the student?

Then it is said again that there is an inherent defect in this theory affecting all moral standards founded on a revelation given once for all. In order that a scheme may be useful for the time for which it is given, it must be of a nature suitable for the time. As a nation evolves, and thousands upon thousands of years pass over the people, we find that that which was suitable for the nation in its infancy becomes unsuitable for the nation in its manhood; many precepts once useful are no longer useful to-day, under the changed circumstances of the time. That difficulty is recognised and met when we come to deal with the Hindu scriptures; for we find there a vast variety of moral teachings suitable for all grades of evolving souls. There are precepts so simple, so clear, so definite, and so imperative, that the youngest of souls may utilise them. But we find also that the Rishis recognised that these precepts were not meant for the training of a highly developed soul. We find in the ancient wisdom that teachings were also given to a few advanced souls, teachings that at the time were utterly unintelligible to the masses. Those teachings were restricted to an inner circle of those who had reached the maturity of the human race. Different schools of morality have always been recognised in Hinduism as necessary for human growth. But whenever, in some great religion, that recognition is not found, you get a certain theoretical morality not suited to the growing needs of the people, and, therefore, there is a sense of unreality, a feeling that it is not reasonable to permit now what was permitted in the infancy of humanity. On the other hand, you find here and there in all scriptures, precepts of the loftiest character which few can even strive to obey. When a command, suitable to the almost savage, is made of universal obligation and is given on the same authority and to the same people as the command given to the saint, there creeps in the feeling of unreality, and confusion of thought is the result.

Another school has arisen, which bases morality on intuition—which says that God speaks to every man through the voice of conscience. It alleges that revelation is made to nation after nation, but that we are not bound by any single book; conscience is the final arbiter. The objection made to this theory is that one man's conscience has the same authority as another man's. If your conscience differs from that of another, then who may decide between conscience and conscience, between the conscience of the ignorant rustic and the conscience of the illuminated mystic? If you say that you admit the principle of evolution, and that you should take as your judge the highest conscience in the race, then intuition fails as a solid basis of morality, and the very element of variety destroys the rock on which you intended to build. The conscience is the voice of the inner man, who remembers the experiences of his past, and out of that immemorial experience judges a given line of conduct to-day. This so-called intuition is the result of countless incarnations, and, according to the number of incarnations, the mind is evolved on which the quality of the conscience of the present individual depends; such intuition, pure and simple, cannot be taken as sufficient guide in morality. We want a commanding voice, not a jangle of tongues. We need the authority of the teacher, and not the confused gabbling of the crowd.

The third school of morality is the school of utilitarianism. That school's view is, as generally presented, neither reasonable nor satisfactory. What is the maxim of this school? "That is right which conduces to the greatest happiness of the greatest number. That is wrong which does not conduce to the greatest happiness of the greatest number." It is a maxim which will not bear analysis. Notice the words "greatest happiness of the greatest number." Such a limitation makes the maxim one which the illuminated intelligence must reject. There is no question of majority when we are dealing with mankind. One life is its root, one God its goal; you cannot separate the happiness of one from that of another. You cannot break up the solid unity, and, picking up the majority, give happiness to them, and leave the minority disregarded. This theory does not recognise the irrefragable unity of the human race, and consequently its maxim fails as a basis of morality. It fails because, in consequence of this unity, one man cannot be perfectly happy unless all men are perfectly happy. His happiness fails in perfection so long as one unit is left out and is unhappy. God does not make distinctions as to units and majorities, but gives one life to humanity and to all creatures. The life of God is the only life in the universe; and the perfect happiness of that life is the goal of the universe.

Then, again, there is a failure in this maxim as an impelling motive because it appeals only to the developed intelligence, that is, to the highly evolved soul. If you go to the ordinary man of the world, to a selfish person, and if you say to that man: "You must lead a life of self-sacrifice, and virtue, and perfect morality, even though the leading it may cost you your life," what do you think would be his answer? Such a man would say: "Why should I do this for the human race, for people in the future whom I shall never see?" If you take this as the standard of right and wrong, then the martyr becomes the greatest fool that humanity has ever produced, for he throws away the possibility of happiness and gets nothing in return. You cannot take this standard, save by limiting your view to the cases in which you get a noble soul, highly developed, and, though not entirely spiritual, with possibility of dawning spirituality. There are such as William Kingdon Clifford, in whose hands the utilitarian doctrine has become inspired with a sublime loftiness of tone. Clifford, in his essay on Ethics, appeals to the highest ideals and gives the noblest teachings of self-sacrifice. He had no belief in the immortality of the soul; approaching death, he could stand beside the grave, believing that that ended all, and preach that the highest virtue is the only thing that a true man can practise, since he owes it to a world which has given him all. But very few will draw inspiration so noble from a prospect so gloomy, and we need a view of right and wrong that shall inspire all, appeal to all, and not merely to those who need its impulse least.

What has come out of all this quarrelling? Confusion, and something worse. A lip-acceptance of revelation, with a practical disregard of it. We have, in fact, a revelation modified by custom. That is the standard which emerges from this confusion. Revelation is taken theoretically as authority, but is disregarded in practice, because often found imperfect. So that you have this unreasonable position, that that which is declared as authority is rejected in the life, and a life of an illogical kind, a happy-go-lucky life, is led, without any logic or reason, without the basis of any definite and rational system.

Can we find in this idea of Dharma a basis more satisfactory, a basis on which the conduct of life may be intelligently built? However low or however high the stage of evolution occupied by the individual, the idea of Dharma gives us the thought of an inner nature unfolding itself in further growth, and we have found that the world is, as a whole, evolving—evolving from the imperfect to the perfect, from the germ to the divine man, stage by stage, in every grade of manifested life. That evolution is by the divine will. God is the moving power, the guiding spirit of the whole. It is His way of building the world. It is the method that He has adopted in order that the spirits that are His children may reproduce the likeness of their Parent. Does not that very statement hint at a law? That is right, which works with the divine purpose in the evolution of the universe, and forwards that evolution from the imperfect to the perfect. That is wrong, which delays or frustrates that divine purpose, and tends to push the universe back to the stage from which it is evolving. It is growing from the mineral to the vegetable, from the vegetable to the animal, from the animal to the animal-man, and from the animal-man to the divine man. That is right, which helps the evolution towards divinity; that is wrong, which drags it backwards or impedes its progress.

Now, if we look for a moment at that idea perhaps we shall acquire a clear view of this law, and no longer feel uneasy over this relative aspect of right and wrong. Place a ladder with its foot on the platform and let it rise to some place beyond the roof. Suppose that one of you had climbed five steps up, another two steps, while a third was standing on the platform. For the man who had climbed up five steps to stand beside the man who was on the second step would be to descend; but for the man on the platform to stand beside the man on the second step would be to ascend. Suppose that every rung of the ladder represents an action: each would be moral and immoral at the same time, according to the point of view from which we look at it. That action which is moral for a brute-man would be immoral for a highly-cultivated man. For a man on the higher rung of the ladder to come down to the lower is to go against evolution, and, therefore, for him such action is immoral; but for a man to rise from the lower stage to stand on that same rung is moral, because it is in the line of his evolution. So that two persons may well stand on the same rung of the ladder, but the one having gone upwards and the other having come downwards to reach it, the action for the one is moral and for the other is immoral. Realise that and we shall begin to find our law.

You have two boys: One of them is a clever and intellectual boy, but is very fond of the gratifications of the body, very fond of food and of anything that gives him sensuous pleasure. The other boy shows some dawning spirituality; he is bright, quick, and intellectual. We will take a third boy who shows the spiritual nature unfolded to a considerable extent. Here are three boys. What motive shall we use to help on the evolution of each? We go to the young man who is very fond of sensual pleasure. If I say to him: "My son, your life should be a life of perfect unselfishness, you should lead an ascetic life," he will shrug his shoulders and go away; and I shall not have helped him up a single rung of the ladder. If I say to him: "My lad, these pleasures of yours are pleasures which give you momentary delight, but they will ruin your body and shatter your health; look on that prematurely old man who has led a life of sensual indulgence; that will be your fate if you go on thus; will it not be better to give a part of your time to the cultivation of your mind, to learning something, so that you may be able to write a book or compose a poem, or help on some of the world's work? You may earn money and get health and fame, and by this attempt you will gratify your ambition; give a rupee now and then to buy a book, instead of buying a dinner." By so addressing him, I stir that youth with an idea of ambition; selfish ambition I admit, but there is not there as yet the power to respond to the appeal for self-sacrifice. The motive of ambition is selfish, but it is selfishness of a higher kind than that of sensual gratification, and as it gives him something of the intellect, raises him out of the brute, puts him on the level of the man who is developing the intellect, and thus helps him to rise higher in the scale of evolution, that is a wiser teaching than the for him impracticable selflessness. It gives him not a perfect ideal, but an ideal suited to his capacity.

But when I come to my intellectual youth with dawning spirituality, I shall put before him the ideal of serving his country, of serving India; I shall make this his object and aim, partly selfish and partly unselfish, thus widening his ambition and helping on his evolution. And when I come to the youth of spiritual nature, I will drop all lower motives, and appeal, on the contrary, to the eternal law of self-sacrifice, to devotion to the one Life, the worship of the great Ones and of God. I shall teach Viveka and Vairagya, and thus help the spiritual nature to unfold its infinite possibilities. Thus, understanding morality as relative, we are able to work effectively. If we fail to help every soul in its own place, it is because we are ill-trained teachers.

In every nation there are certain definite things which are marked as wrong, such as murder, theft, lying, vileness. All these are recognised as crimes. That is the general view. But it is not wholly borne out by facts. How far are these things recognised as moral and how far as immoral in practice? Why are they recognised as wrong? Because the masses of the nation have reached a certain stage of evolution. Because the majority of the nation are at about the same level of growth, and at that level they recognise these things as evil, as against progress. The result is that the minority, being below this stage, is regarded as being made up of "criminals." The majority has reached a higher stage of evolution, and the majority makes the law; then those who cannot come up even to the lowest level of the majority are dubbed criminals. Two types of criminals present themselves to our view. One type upon which we cannot make any impression by appealing to their sense of right and wrong. They are spoken of by the ignorant public as hardened criminals. But this view is a mistaken one, and leads to lamentable results. They are merely ignorant ungrown souls, child-souls, infants in the school of life, and we do not help them to grow by trampling them down and brutalising them further, because they are scarcely a grade removed from the brute. We should use all the means in our power, all that our reason can suggest, to guide and teach these child-souls, to discipline them into a better life; let us not treat them as hardened criminals because they are mere babies in the nursery.

The other type of criminals is made up of those who feel a certain amount of remorse and repentance after the commission of a crime: who know that they have done wrong. They stand on a higher level and can be helped to resist evil in future by the very suffering imposed on them by human law. I spoke of the necessity of all experience, in order that the soul might learn to discern between right and wrong. We need experience of good and evil until we can discriminate the good from the evil, *but no further*. The moment the two lines of actions are distinct before you, and you know that the one is right and the other is wrong, then if you choose the wrong road you are committing sin, you are going against a law that you know and admit. A man at this stage commits sin, because his desires are strong, prompting him to choose the path which is wrong. He suffers, and it is well that he should suffer, if he follows these desires. The moment the knowledge of wrong is present there, at that moment also there is deliberate degradation in yielding to the impulse. Experience of the wrong is only needed before the wrong is recognised as wrong, and in order that it may come to be so recognised. When two courses are before a man, neither of which appears to him to be morally different from the other, then he may take either of those courses and commit no wrong. But the moment a thing is known to be wrong, it is a treason to ourselves to allow the brute in us to overpower the God in us. That is what is really sin; that is what is the condition of most, but not all, wrong-doers to-day.

Let us pass from that and look at some particular faults a little more closely. Take murder: we find that the common sense of the community makes a distinction between killing and killing. If a man takes up a knife in anger and stabs his enemy, the law calls him a murderer and hangs him. If a thousand men take up knives and stab a thousand men, then the killing is called war. Glory, and not punishment, is awarded to him who thus kills. The same crowd who hoot the murderer of one enemy, cheer the men who have killed ten thousand enemies. What is this strange anomaly? How can we explain it? Is there anything to justify the verdict of the community? Is there any distinction between the two acts which justifies the difference of treatment? There is. War is a thing against which the public conscience more and more protests, and in a moment we shall have to look at this fact of the growth of the public conscience. But while we should do all we can to prevent war, should try to spread peace and to educate our children in the love of peace, there is none the less a real distinction between the conduct of one who kills through private malice, and the killing which takes place in war;

this difference is so far-reaching that I shall dilate upon it a little. In the one case, a personal grudge is satisfied, and a personal satisfaction is found. In the other case, one man in killing another man is not gratifying a personal feeling, is serving no personal object, is seeking no personal gain. The men are killing each other as an act of obedience to a command laid on them by their superiors, whose is the responsibility for the righteousness of the war. All my life I have preached peace, and I have striven to show the evils of war. But, none the less, I recognise that there is much in the mere discipline of the military force which is of vital importance to those who are subjected to that training. What does the soldier learn? He learns obedience to order, cleanliness, quickness, accuracy, promptness in action, and willingness to undergo physical hardships without complaint or murmur. He learns to risk his life and to give it for an ideal cause. Is not that a training which has its place in the evolution of the soul? Does not the soul profit by this training? When the ideal of the country fires the heart, when life is sacrificed for it gladly by rough, common, and uneducated men, they may be rude, violent, drunken, but they are passing through a training, which, in lives to come, will make them better and nobler men.

Then take a phrase used by an Englishman of somewhat strange genius, Rudyard Kipling, who makes soldiers say that they will fight "for the widow at Windsor." That may sound a little rough, but it is well for the man who starves, who suffers mutilation on the battlefield, if he sees before him his Queen-Empress, mother of millions of people, and offers up his life to her, learning for the first time the beauty of fidelity, of courage, and devotion. There is the distinction which, very dimly grasped by the public, marks the distinction between private killing and war. For the interest of the one is personal; that of the other belongs to a wider self—the self of the nation.

In dealing with this question of morality, we fall often practically below that view. There are many cases of theft, of lying, of killing, that the law of man does not punish, but that the law of karma notes and brings back to the doer. Many an act of theft is disguised as commerce; many an act of cheating is disguised as trade; many a fine arrangement of lies is classified as diplomacy. Crime reappears under startling forms, disguised and hidden, and men have to learn self-purification in life after life. Then comes in another consideration, before we come to the essence of sin—one which I cannot entirely overpass—thought and action. There are some actions which a man commits which are inevitable. You do not understand what you are doing when you allow yourself to think along a line of wrong. You covet in thought another man's gold; you are grasping with your mind's hands at every moment what is not yours. You are building the Dharma of the thief. The inner nature, the interior nature, is Dharma, and if you build that inner nature by thoughts that are evil, you will be born with the Dharma that will carry you to deeds of vice. Those deeds will be done without thought. Have you any idea how many thoughts in you have already gone towards the making of an action? You may dam up water and prevent it from flowing along a channel, but the moment a hole is made in the dam, the pent-up water will flow through the hole and sweep the dam away. So is it with thought and action. Thought accumulates slowly behind the dam of absence of opportunity. As you think and think, the stream of thought grows fuller and fuller behind the breastwork of circumstances. In another life that breastwork of circumstances gives way, and the action is committed before any new thought has occurred. Those are the inevitable crimes, which sometimes blast a great career, when the thought of the past finds its fruitage in the present, when the karma of accumulated thought comes forth as action. If the opportunity comes to you, and you have time to pause, time to say, "Shall I do it?" then that action is not inevitable for you. The pause for thought means that you can put the thought on the other side, and so strengthen the barrier. There is no excuse for doing an action which you have thought of as wrong. Those actions only are inevitable which are done without thinking, where the thought belongs to the past and the action to the present.

We come now to the great question of separateness:—there lies in every deed the essence of wrong. In the past separateness was right. The great course of the divine life-stream was dividing itself into multiplicity; it was needed to build up individual centres of consciousness. So long as a centre needs strengthening, separateness is on the side of progress. Souls at one period need to be selfish; they cannot do without selfishness in the early stages of growth. But now the law of progressing life for the more advanced is the outgrowing of separateness, and the seeking to realise unity. We are now on the path towards unity; we are approaching nearer and nearer to each other. We must now unite, in order to grow further. The purpose is the same, though the method has changed in the evolution through the ages. The public conscience is beginning to recognise that not in separateness but in unity there lies the true growth of a nation. We are trying to substitute arbitration for war, co-operation for competition, protection of the weak for trampling them under foot, and all this, because the line of evolution now goes towards unity and not towards separateness. Separation is the mark of descent into matter, and unification is the mark of the ascent to spirit. The world is on the upward trend, although thousands of souls may lag behind. The ideal now is for peace, co-operation, protection, brotherhood, and helpfulness. The essence of sin now lies in separateness.

But that thought leads us on to another test of conduct. Is the action we are doing one which seeks our own gain, or which helps on the general good? Is our life a self-seeking useless life, or does it help humanity? If it is selfish, then it is wrong, it is evil, it is against the growth of the world. If you be among those who have seen the beauty of the ideal of unity, and have recognised the perfection of the divine manhood that we seek, then you should kill out this heresy of separateness in yourself.

When we look at much of the teaching of the past and see the conduct of the sages, certain questions in morality arise, which some find it rather hard to answer. I raise this question here, because I may suggest to you the line of thought by which you may defend the Shâstras from carping critics, and which may enable you to profit by their teachings, without becoming confused. A great sage is not always, in his conduct, an example that an ordinary man should endeavour to follow. When I speak now of a great sage, I mean one in whom all personal desire is dead, who is not attracted to any object in the world, whose only life is in obedience to the divine will, who gives himself as one of the channels of divine force for the helping of the world. He performs the functions of a God, and the functions of the Gods differ much from the functions of men. The earth is full of all kinds of catastrophes—wars, earthquakes, famine, pestilences, plagues. Who is their cause? There is no cause in God's universe save God Himself, and these things which seem so terrible, so shocking, so painful, are His ways of teaching us when we are going wrong. A plague sweeps off thousands of the men of a nation. A mighty war scatters its thousands of dead on the field of carnage. Why? Because that nation had disregarded the divine law of its growth, and must learn its lesson by suffering, if it will not learn it by reason. Plague is the result of disregarding the laws of health and of clean living. God is too merciful to permit a law to be disregarded by the whims and fancies and feelings of slowly evolving man, without calling attention to the disregard. These catastrophes are worked by the Gods, by the agents of Îshvara, who, invisible throughout the world, administer the divine law, as a magistrate administers the civil laws. Just because they are administrators of the law, and are acting impersonally, their actions are no more examples for us to follow than the action of the judge in imprisoning a criminal is an example to show that an ordinary man may take revenge on his enemy. Look, for instance, at the great sage Nârada. We find him stirring up war when two nations have reached a point where the higher good of each can only be gained by the struggles of war and by the conquest of one by the other. Bodies are killed, and it is the best help to the men thus slain that their bodies should be struck away, and that, in new bodies, they may have greater possibility of growth. Gods bring about the battle in which thousands of men are slain. It would be wicked for us to imitate them, because to stir up war for the sake of conquest, or gain, or ambition, or for some object where personality comes in, is sinful. But in the case of Nârada it is not so, because Devarshis such as he is are helping the world along the path of evolution by striking away the obstacles. You will understand something of the wonders and mysteries of the universe when you know that things that seem evil from the side of form are good from the side of life; all that happens is working for the best. "There *is* a divinity that shapes our ends, rough hew them how we will." Religion is right when it says that the Gods rule over the world and guide nations, and lead and even scourge them into the right path when they go astray.

A man, full of personality and attracted by the objects of desire, whose whole self is Kâma, such a man, committing an action instigated by Kâma, often commits a crime; but the very same action committed by a liberated soul, free from all desire, in carrying out the divine order, would be rightly done. In the utter disbelief that men have fallen into as to the working of the Gods, such words may seem strange, but there is no energy in nature which is not the physical manifestation of a God carrying out the will of the Supreme. That is the true view of nature. We see the side of form and, blinded by Mâyâ, call it evil; but the Gods, as they break up forms, are clearing away every obstacle that obstructs the way of evolution.

We may here understand one or two of those other questions that are often thrown in our faces by those who take a superficial view of things. Supposing a man, who is longing to commit a sin, is prevented from committing it solely by the pressure of circumstances; suppose that the longing is growing stronger and stronger; what is the best thing for him? To have an opportunity to put his longing into action. To commit a crime? Yes, even a crime is less injurious to the soul than a continued brooding over it in the mind, the growing of a cancer at the heart of life. An action once done is dead, and the suffering that follows it teaches the needed lesson, but thought is generative and living.* Do you understand that? If you do, then you will also understand why you find in the scriptures a God putting in the way of a man an opportunity of committing the sin that man is longing to commit, and in fact is committing in his heart. He will suffer, no doubt, for his sin, but he will learn by the suffering that falls on the wrong-doer. Had that evil thought been left to grow in the heart, it would have grown stronger and stronger, and would have gradually wrecked the whole moral nature of the man. For it is like a cancer which, if not speedily removed, will poison the whole body. Far more merciful it is, that such a man should sin and suffer pain, than that he should long to sin and be held back by lack of opportunity merely, and thus make inevitable degradation for lives to come.

So also if a man is making rapid progress, and there is a hidden weakness in him, or some past Karma not exhausted, or evil deed not expiated, that man cannot be liberated while that Karma

* This does not mean that a man should commit a sin rather than struggle against it. So long as he struggles, it is well with him, and he is gaining strength. The case referred to is where there is no struggle, but where the man is longing to do the action and only lacks opportunity. In such case, the sooner the opportunity comes, the better for the man; the pent-up longing breaks forth, the realised wish brings suffering, the man learns a necessary lesson, and is purged of an ever-increasing moral poison.

remains unexhausted, while there is a debt still unpaid. What is the most merciful thing to do? To help that man to pay his debt in anguish and degradation, so that the misery following on the fault may exhaust the Karma of the past. It means that there is swept out of his way an obstacle that prevents its liberation, and God puts that temptation in his way to break the last barrier down. I have not time to work out the details of this most pregnant line of thought, but I ask you to follow it for yourselves and see what it means, and how it illuminates the dark problems of growth, the falls of the saints.

If, when you have assimilated it, you then read such a book as the *Mahâbhârata*, you will understand the workings of the Gods in the affairs of men; you will see the Gods working in storm and sunshine, in peace and in war, and you will know that it is well with the man and with the nation, whatever may occur to them; for the noblest wisdom and the tenderest love are guiding them to their appointed goal.

I come now to the last word—a word I will dare to speak to you who have been listening to me patiently on a subject so difficult and abstruse. There is a yet higher note: know that there is a supreme goal, and the last steps on the path to it are not the steps where Dharma can any longer guide us. Let us take some wonderful words from the great Teacher, Shrî Krishṇa, and let us see how in His final instruction He speaks of something loftier than anything on which we have dared to touch. Here is His message of peace: "Listen thou again to My supreme word, most secret of all; beloved art thou of Me, and steadfast of heart, therefore will I speak for thy benefit. Merge thy Manas in Me, be my devotee, sacrifice to Me, prostrate thyself before Me, thou shalt come even to Me. Abandoning all Dharmas, come unto Me alone for shelter; sorrow not, I will liberate thee from all sins." *

My last words are addressed only to those who lead here a life of supreme longing to sacrifice themselves; they have a right to these last words of hope and peace. Then the end of Dharma is reached. Then the man desires no longer anything save the Lord. When the soul has reached that stage of evolution where it asks nothing of the world, but gives itself wholly to God, when it has outgrown all the promptings of desire, when the heart has gained freedom by love, when the whole being throws itself forward at the feet of the Lord—then abandon you all Dharmas; they are no longer for you; no longer for you the law of growth, no longer for you that balancing of duty, no longer for you that scrutiny of conduct. You have given yourself to the Lord.

* *Bhagavad Gîtâ*, xviii. 64–66.

There is nothing left in you that is not divine. What Dharma can any longer remain for you, for, united to Him, you are no longer a separated self. Your life is hid in Him, His life is yours; you may be living in the world, you are but His instruments. You are His wholly. Your life is Îshvara's, and Dharma has no longer any claim on you. Your devotion has liberated you, for your life is hid in God. That is the word of the Teacher. That is the last thought I would leave with you.

And now, my brothers, farewell. Our work together is done. After this imperfect presentation of a mighty subject, may I say to you: listen to the thought in the message, and not to the speaker who is the messenger; open your hearts to the thought, and forget the imperfection of the lips that have spoken it. Remember that as we climb to God, we must need try, however feebly, to pass on to our brothers some touch of that life we reach after. Forget therefore the speaker, but remember the teaching. Forget the imperfections which are in the messenger, not in the message. Worship the God whose teaching we have been studying, and pardon in your charity the faults of the servant who has given it utterance.

PEACE TO ALL BEINGS.

PRINTED BY NEILL AND CO., LTD., EDINBURGH.